DATING
AMY

DATING
AMY
50 TRUE
Confessions
of a Serial Dater

Amy DeZellar

WARNER BOOKS

NEW YORK BOSTON

This is a work of nonfiction, but all the names (and in some cases, occupations) have been changed in order to protect the anonymity of the characters.

5 Spot

Hachette Book Group USA
1271 Avenue of the Americas
New York, NY 10020

5 Spot is an imprint of Warner Books, Inc.
The 5 Spot name and logo are trademarks of Warner Books, Inc.

Printed in the United States of America

First Edition: June 2006
10 9 8 7 6 5 4 3 2 1

Warner Books is a trademark of Time Inc. Used under license.

Library of Congress Cataloging-in-Publication Data
DeZellar, Amy.
   Dating Amy : 50 true confessions of a serial dater /
Amy DeZellar.—1st ed.
     p. cm.
   ISBN-13: 978-0-446-69654-8
   ISBN-10: 0-446-69654-4
   1. Dating (Social customs)—Anecdotes. 2. DeZellar, Amy—Relations
with men. I. Title: Fifty true confessions of a serial dater. II. Title.
HQ801.D5 2006
306.73—dc22   2005037194

For the other hopeless romantics
and eternal optimists

Acknowledgments

Thanks to my agents Jenny Bent and Melissa Flashman and my editor Karen Kosztolnyik.

Thanks also to Michele Bidelspach, Holly Henderson Root, Penny, Kurt Knutsson, ABC News, the crew from TechTV, and everyone who let me write about them.

Special thanks to Darren Jones, who patiently helped me every step of the way, and to all the readers of DatingAmy.com, especially those who sent money, and to my parents for their unbridled encouragement of my creativity regardless of cost and inconvenience (to them, not me).

Most of all I want to thank the men of the fifty dates—the good, the bad, and the so bad they were good—without whom this book would never have happened.

Contents

Introduction

More and more it seems that sex involves saddles, stilettos, and schoolgirl outfits, but my only love-life fetish is writing about it.

Even that is new for me, because while I sometimes wear as little as possible, emotionally I am anything but an exhibitionist. My motivation for writing a book about my dating Web site was that there are just some things you can't say on the Internet. My motivation for documenting fifty dates on a Web site in the first place was strictly financial. That's how it started out, anyway.

I optimistically thought I could take two wildly disparate elements—personal writing and being well paid for it—and combine them. I was sure that the Internet would give me enough exposure to land me a great job. I wanted to be wading in money while not compromising my artistic vision.

For years, reconciling the desire for art with the desire for money had haunted my career like a needy ghost I couldn't break up with. I had been a pop-culture writer in Los Angeles, moved to Seattle the year before, and hadn't worked since. There just wasn't room for yet another person to write about bands and movies and restaurants in my new city unless you knew someone, and I didn't.

Desperation about my career was becoming like an alarm clock whose buzzer keeps getting louder the longer you sleep in. First I worried about artistic fulfillment. I'm fascinated by men since I know nothing about them, so I pitched a fun dating column

1

called "Single Latte" to the *Seattle Times* and was met with complete silence. Next I worried about getting any sort of writing work, artistically fulfilling or otherwise, and applied to be a reporter for a trade magazine about fish. After I didn't get that job I started worrying about cash, because I didn't have any left.

I just knew that if I could get some notoriety I would land a great job. That's what I told myself, anyway. My career up until then had been rocky at best. It seemed that whether I worked for a start-up dot-com or an established business, things eventually ended with me weeping and holding a cardboard box in my arms as I pushed the down button on the elevator with my elbow. Although it was never my fault, I had been laid off several times in a row and it was getting demoralizing.

I had the same dreamy desire for the perfect blend of art and commerce in a man, too.

I wanted a barefoot poet with tousled shoulder-length hair and skin as soft as the faded cotton shirts he wore, but he had to be great at business and have piles of money so he could support our tastes for gourmet food, fine wines, and my hobby, lying around on the couch thinking up interesting thoughts. I also wanted him to cook, share my love of horror movies, and not notice other women.

It reminded me of the Barbie doll that I bought at an antique store two Christmases ago to auction on eBay. Her abnormally perfect body would be 39-18-33 if she were real, and researchers in Helsinki have determined that she would have 15 percent body fat. Barbie has an ever-increasing designer wardrobe, houses, cars, and the undying devotion of both Ken and GI Joe. I have an apartment, the #18 bus, and no boyfriend. My only designer clothes are from thrift stores and therefore accidental. The only thing Barbie and I have in common is a thirty-nine-inch bust.

My particular Barbie didn't seem to have very good taste,

though. She was clad in a modest robin's egg blue two-piece swimsuit and a black velvet choker with matching onyx-and-gold earrings. It was kind of dressy jewelry for a day of beach frolicking, even in Barbie's confetti-and-sequins world. Her eclectic taste in accessorizing was explained when I checked the dates on her back. Her body was a vintage 1966, but her head was a decade younger: its stamp said 1976. She was a Frankenbarbie. A child somewhere had had the idea that she could make a better doll by taking part of one and forcing it onto part of another. Plop. Who cares if the choker didn't go with the swimwear?

I understood the unknown child's impulse because my whole life I had mentally done that with men. If I could just take Karl the Artist's sensitivity and unique worldview and combine them with Jason the Banker's ability to turn any idea into money, I'd have the perfect guy. I'd better throw in Rick's sense of fidelity, though.

While I was certain what I wanted in a man, I had basically made it to my late thirties with absolutely no idea what I wanted in a relationship. Cross-dressing musicians, circus performers, philosophy grad students—I had always dated purely for my own entertainment. I had only had a handful of boyfriends in my whole life, and had never considered marrying any of them, but instead had dated randomly and with an open-minded verve that embraced every kind of man, regardless of income, prospects, or mental state.

Though I had never written about relationships, analyzing them was tantamount to an avocation for me. I'm as naturally curious and tactless as yet another unknown child—the little kid in "The Emperor's New Clothes" who points out that His Highness is stark naked. I simply cannot stand by and listen to some idiot spout off bad information, unless that idiot is me. I'm constantly debunking dating myths (or bunking them, if I agree), usually in my head but sometimes aloud if the person is spewing especially unhelpful clichés like "Love only happens when you're not looking for it."

"Tasha is such a nice person, she really deserves a relationship," someone will say. "I don't think it's a meritocracy, most serial killers and politicians are married," I'll point out. I'm a realist (when it comes to other people's love lives anyway) and you'll never hear me use terms like *soul mate* except ironically.

Then I got what seemed like a good idea at the time: Why don't I look for a boyfriend and document it on the Internet? I'm in a strange city, and stories about a person's descent into madness are always popular, and, if nothing else, maybe I could find a shoulder not only to cry on but to take me out to dinner. Maybe the sheer public-ness of my search would humiliate me into finding some sort of romantic direction.

The result of all this was Dating Amy, my literal labor of love.

My name is Amy. I'm going on fifty dates and I'm taking you with me . . . but only if you promise not to whine "Are we there yet?"

DATE 1 The Blind Date

TRUE CONFESSION

I wasn't sure about meeting this odd man from Match.com, and, truth be told, I wouldn't have if I hadn't already launched the Web site and therefore needed a date to write about.

Autumn. The snap in the air, leaves the color of flames, a holiday that includes dressing up and not buying gifts for other people—it's my absolute favorite season. Jews consider it the beginning of the new year. I'm not Jewish, but am often mistaken for such with my pale olive skin, dark hair, and what I tell myself is a dry, Woody Allen–circa-*Manhattan*–style wit that doesn't go over that well in Seattle where I live. Fall has always seemed like a time of new beginnings to me, too. It was the perfect season to launch the dating Web site that I was sure would launch my career, and I was going on my very first date for it. I felt like a sophomore girl getting asked to the homecoming dance by a senior, except that I was in my late thirties and the senior was some stranger from Match.com and we probably wouldn't have dated under normal circumstances.

Our abnormal circumstances were that, (1) as bold as I am about some things, I don't believe in asking men out, and (2) he asked me out through an old ad I had up on Match.com just when I needed a date.

DatingAmy.com was not much more than a home page that

said "I flip between dating men who are like George Costanza and men who are like George Clooney . . . then quickly back again. If romance is a numbers game, it only makes sense for me to pick a biggish number." The bizarre pressure of needing a date to write about on the Internet was standing in front of me like a fat woman in a bright orange suit holding a Drive Slowly sign as I trundled past, a single person in the diamond lane.

Driving, slowly or otherwise, was apparently something my date did not have to worry about.

"Sorry I won't be picking you up," his e-mail said. "I can't drive. I'll explain when I meet you. It's not that I am a loser, though." Hmmm, that last part would be up to me, surely. "If he can't drive it means too many DUIs or he's on parole," my friends assured me. "He sounds great!"

Like most people, I'm always nervous to meet a blind date. Unlike most people, it's not because I think he may not like me or think I'm attractive; I'm much more worried about what I'll think of him. Part of my hesitation—I thought pretty realistic in this case—was that he had sent a picture of himself with five cats on his head and a story from his childhood about a fish flopping in a wooden boat that was somehow supposed to be analogous to meeting me. "Maybe after we meet you can tell me what I'm doing wrong with dating," he wrote hopefully. I was starting a list already.

We had agreed to meet at a pub and barbecue place whose rotating sign features an apparently not-too-bright pig and cow dancing arm in arm. As soon as I stepped inside, a fortyish man with a shaved head, one dangly earring, and glasses as thick as mason jar bottoms wheeled around on his stool at the bar and asked if I was Amy. He was having a pint of beer with a lemon slice floating in it and ordered a chardonnay for me.

Although it was *Monday Night Football* time, the TV in front of us was tuned to a sailing event. "Have you been watching this?" I asked.

"Well, not exactly," he answered.

He went on to apologize for not picking me up but explained that he can't drive because he is vision impaired. Really vision impaired.

Jesus, my blind date was actually blind.

When you're doing online dating, it's perfectly understandable to shave a few numbers off your age or weight and add them to your height. Less forgivable, but still in the ballpark, is putting up a picture that's a year or two old, but how could someone omit the fact that they're missing one of the senses? There are only five of them and sight is one of the important ones. For example, I guess I don't really care if someone I'm involved with has a sense of taste. Sure, I'd feel bad for him and touring wine country might be less fun with him, but ultimately it wouldn't affect me personally. Someone's not being able to see feels completely different and like something that's at least worth mentioning.

"Four really gorgeous blonde girls walked in just before you did," he said. "I told the bartender I am definitely coming *here* again."

I looked around and didn't see any girls, gorgeous, blonde, or otherwise. Normally I would take that kind of a comment so early into a blind date as a very bad sign about where things were heading, but given the circumstances I decided to let it go.

He mentioned the cats I had seen pictured sitting on his head. They were all his, obviously. He said that sometimes he wished that he could be lord of the manor, like in a Gothic novel, and that someone else—a servant of some sort—would attend to the demanding cats and their needs. From that point on I thought of him as Indentured by Cats. Well, as that and also as that blind guy who didn't mention he was blind.

"Have you noticed how people put those tacky tchotchkes by the side of the road at accident sites as a tribute to their loved ones who died there?" I floundered for a topic to try to put his handicap into perspective. "I guess nothing says, 'We cannot accept that you were cruelly swept off the planet at such a young age' like Beanie Babies and Mylar balloons. In Germany they make crosses and things out of the twisted wreckage of the actual cars to mark the spot."

"Of the European countries I like Holland the best; it's like a second home to me," he said, thankfully not completely picking up the conversational thread I had started. He raved about how great the Dutch are. I didn't comment but silently recalled an incident at a train station in Amsterdam when I changed my mind about a ticket and the agent threw a golf pencil at me and screamed, "IS THIS HOW YOU DO THINGS IN YOUR OWN COUNTRY?" Never mind that the answer to that question is, of course, yes, the experience left me scarred.

As Indentured told me about himself, I learned that he is quite accomplished and lives a rich life, each facet of which is punctuated by beautiful women:

He is a businessman. He's an entrepreneur, really, as he owns his own business. He and his employees enjoy a sort of stalled adolescence akin to the guys in John Cusack's record store in *High Fidelity*. Their workday consists of Yoda in-jokes, computer games that may or may not include real-life reenactments, and the hiring of cute chicks whenever possible.

He is also a dirty old man. He told me about getting suggestive e-mails from women on Match.com who would never need to post on the Internet to get dates. "I guess it seems too good to be true that a twenty-one-year-old who is working her way through medical school by lingerie modeling is interested in me and 'up for anything,' but I click on the link to her Web site anyway. It's always porn or a hooker."

He talked about a thirty-year-old he had beers with for five hours and how he spilled a beer on her. He called the next day and she told him he was too old and too bald and that she wasn't attracted to him, couldn't he *see* that? Despite the unfortunate word choice on her part, I couldn't help but admire the woman's decisiveness. Unlike me, she knew what she wanted in a man and she wasn't afraid to say so.

I constantly second-guess myself. Should I have given this one more of a chance? Am I too concerned with feeling chemistry right away and not allowing it time to grow? Should I lower my looks standards? How about my income requirements? Is this guy going to be the best I ever do? I mean one's dating pool has to dry up someday and there will be a point in every person's life when they do indeed date the best person they're ever going to get. If they don't end up with that person, it will all be downhill from there, by definition. And so on.

The blind man told me all about speed dating, where singles sit at tables for two and everyone talks for seven minutes, then a buzzer goes off and they switch partners until everyone has "dated" everyone else. He said that there were ringers when he did it—again, girls so beautiful they would never have to do something like speed dating. He complained to the hostess of the event that it was unfair. He had taken a cab there and the only good-looking women were her friends and not really available. He argued that it was discrimination against the handicapped. It took me a beat to realize that by "handicapped" he meant other than socially, since as the owner of a business he had built from the ground up and a social life replete with beautiful women, he was doing better than most of my guy friends and they can all see.

Normally I loathe hearing about how beautiful other women are, especially from a potential prospect. It's even worse when he doesn't have one kind thing to say about my looks. This particular situation had me in a politically correct quandary, though. On the one hand, he was just another guy yammering on about hot chicks right in front of my face. On the other hand, he was blind.

I couldn't help but be fascinated by his very male sense of entitlement.

It truly pointed up a core difference between men and women. If a blind woman were on a date with a stranger, she'd probably feel by turns hesitant and humble—assuming she would even have the confidence to do something like online dating, which is scary even when you have all of your senses. She would certainly have mentioned it, probably apologetically, before the date. Leave it to a man to act like the world is his own private beauty contest even if he needs the program printed up in Braille. In a way I admired him.

My political correctness held my sense of self at bay for the better part of an hour until I finally broke: "How do you know all these women are so beautiful?" I asked. "You're blind."

"I'm not *that* blind," he said.

When I was ready to leave he asked me to wait with him because he wouldn't be able to see the bright yellow taxi when it drove up. I'm sure if there were a gorgeous blonde driving it he'd be able to spot it.

After I saw him off, I stopped at the grocery store to pick up a Lean Cuisine on my way home since he hadn't offered dinner. Tiny, ornamental pumpkins sat like fat orange jewels in the front bins. Fall had arrived and I felt good. The date had gone well, and despite his oddness, or maybe because of it, I had had fun with Indentured by Cats, and when he asked me out again, I said yes. More important, my dating project had officially started.

It had started to drizzle, so I'd put on a baseball cap I'd bought on vacation. "You're wearing a Yankees hat in Seattle? We need to talk," the young guy behind the checkout said. He was tall, big, athletic, confident. A wave of chemicals crashed over me and then receded, the undertow pulling the sand from underneath my toes. "What's your name?" he said. "I see you in here all the time."

In the span of a few hours it seemed that I had seen the difference between the kind of man I was going to be dating and the kind of man I was attracted to.

BUNK DEBUNK

Myth: Love only happens when you're not looking for it.

Debunked!

I always suspect a death wish—or rather celibacy wish—coming from the people giving this advice. Invariably they are also the sorts who panic if they are alone for more than a week and who met their most recent liaison by placing ads on more than one dating Web site.

Really, when I'm "not looking" for anyone, it means that on the rare occasions I do leave the house, I give one-word answers to strangers and haven't washed my hair.

Of course you have to be looking for love; it's a completely different mind-set from not looking. And not looking is not pretty, in my case at least.

DATE 2 The Accidental Interview

TRUE CONFESSION
I wanted my dates to be in the morning paper, but not like this.

The reporter was peering at my literally blind date, Indentured by Cats, over her gold wire-rimmed glasses, pen poised over a tiny notebook. He and I were at a tasting being held at a wine store and we were cornered.

"Would you say this is a romantic place to take someone? I mean, is this a date?"

Please pretend you're deaf too, I thought.

"I don't know, *is* this a date?" he said, and they both turned to me.

"It is," he quickly answered for me.

"I'm writing an article on wine tasting for the travel section of the *Seattle Times.*"

Of course she was, because the editor over there won't even answer my e-mails about my dating column idea, so now somehow Bad Luck and Irony have gotten together and found someone to accidentally interview me about one of my dates while I'm actually on the date with a man who doesn't even know I have a dating Web site.

"I have my own column," she continued.

Of course she did.

"Can I get your occupation?"

Unemployed, thanks for the reminder.

"Web site editor," I answered.

". . . and the spelling of your name?"

M-O-R-T-I-F-I-E-D, I thought.

"A-M-Y," I answered instead.

Things had been going very well up until that point. Indentured had taken care of everything—he knew the owner and brought special wineglasses for us and was on time.

The featured wines were from New Zealand, as was the guy pouring them. Apparently Monty Python had a bit about Australian wines, which Indentured and the pourer were able to reenact and which was probably funnier thirty years ago when it came out, because Australia didn't export wines then. I did like the part where they said Perth Pink "is a bottle with a message in it, and the message is 'Beware,'" though.

I was having a great time. Everything was lovely. The pinot noir was outstanding. Indentured didn't think I saw him sneak into line to buy me a bottle after I raved about it.

Later on he took me to dinner at a romantic continental supper club around the corner. Though I tried not to show it, I was still bothered by getting interviewed. I wanted my dates written about in the paper, but in my Pulitzer fantasy they were usually written by me. I could barely concentrate on my jerk chicken with puréed sweet potato, sautéed spinach, and two glasses of Australian chardonnay. He presented me with the bottle of pinot noir. He is bright, if very focused on nerdlike things like computer games. He explained the baby at the end of *2001: A Space Odyssey* for about ten minutes and I still didn't get it, but that demonstrated that he possessed the quality of patience. Maybe I could get used to being like Mrs. Wonder or Mrs. Charles . . . or someone married to a nonblack, non–musical-genius who was blind.

I could definitely see some benefits to getting involved with him. I would be able to lie about my appearance for one thing. Sweats and T-shirts could pose as respectable clothing until they started to smell funny. Beauty routines like getting highlights or my hair trimmed would certainly be less urgent. Nail polish would be rendered obsolete.

After dinner, Indentured and I walked across the street to a European wine bar where he had champagne and I had peppermint tea. He began talking about the aftermath of his divorce. He admitted his complete surprise that the hauntingly beautiful twenty-somethings who bartend at his neighborhood pub didn't pursue him once he stopped wearing his wedding ring. He thought the gold band was all that was standing between him and unbridled ecstasy, and did not consider that their eager politeness may have been tip-motivated rather than lust-based.

He told a long story of a disappointing trip he and his then-wife took to Tuscany while I watched my tea bag slowly turn in the white ceramic cup. "Divorce is so discouraging because you're basically admitting that things didn't work out with the coolest person you've ever dated," he said. I had never thought of it that way. Maybe I was reading him all wrong. Maybe he was sensitive and deep and not just some horny blind guy with a sense of entitlement who read social signals poorly.

"I couldn't wait to get out of my marriage because I wanted to nail the good-looking girls who work at the coffee shop near my house. They were always flirting with me when I was married. When they said hello and remembered that I like double lattes, I could just tell they wanted me too. Once I was divorced they weren't as interested as I thought, though."

Or maybe I was reading him perfectly. I felt the need to defend myself as a never-married. "Married people are kind of arrogant to think they'd all be doing so well if they were single. I mean, what does that say for people who actually are single and can't find anyone? That we're all just losers and you wouldn't be in our circumstance for long if you were single?"

"Well, is that the case?" he said.

The techno music and cosmopolitan feel of the wine bar reminded me of L.A. and made me lonely for the people I used to know there. That melancholy feeling hits swiftly and hard when you don't have a lot of friends in town. When it was time to go, his big yellow taxi pulled up. I live two blocks from the wine bar and his cab was going past my apartment, but he did not offer me a ride, although he did sort of make me kiss him, which was awkward. It was like I was the guy seeing his girl safely home by putting her in a cab.

Later that week when I told him I didn't feel we were a match he said he was disappointed, as I was sweet and easy to be with, but he couldn't afford to keep dating me anyway. I felt bad because he seemed to like me, but I also felt that he didn't know me at all. I was once again thinking I had misjudged him when he said, "I was watching *South Park* the other night and I wished you were with me. I know how much we both love it."

He was confusing me with some other woman obviously, perhaps a gorgeous blonde twenty-one-year-old from the Internet. I don't watch *South Park*.

Wait, how does he watch *South Park*?

BUNK DEBUNK

Myth: If I were single I'd be with any number of people I can tell are dying for me.

Debunked!

This largely improbable phrase is only uttered by people who've been in a relationship for a very long time. The implication is that these married/committed people would be much better at being single than a single person is. When you're in a relationship, anyone of the opposite sex who is nice to you becomes a potential prospect since it's all fantasy. The men at work who ask if you want to grab a bite, your friend's husband who tells you that you look great, the client who brings you a latte and laughs at your jokes—to the mind of the spoken-for these are all tantamount to a promise ring.

Those of us who are single know better. For one thing, if you're taken, you're safe, so any commitment-phobic or sexually confused person you know will be drawn to you like a metal filing to a magnet. Most of the people you think are interested in you would in actuality run away like the knights in *Monty Python and the Holy Grail* if they thought there was any chance at all of being with you.

If you were single, you'd find out soon enough how hard it is to find a truly committed relationship. That's why single people are always saying how hard it is to find a truly committed relationship. It's not that we're all losers who don't get it. Really.

I'll never forget having lunch with a friend who's been married since college. "Look at this young guy coming over," she said with a smug smile. "I have this happen all the time."

It was the waiter.

DATE 3   There's a Penis Loose in the Cornfield

TRUE CONFESSION

Originally called "A Goat and Two Beatles," this is a cautionary tale of how an innocent trip to a pumpkin patch can go horribly awry when one or more members of the party become engorged.

Last summer I met Have Glitter Ball Will Travel, a lounge singer from New York, at a coffee shop on a Sunday morning. It was a blind date we had set up through the Internet. Me: dark pink camisole from Victoria's Secret, black shorts, tanned legs. Him: one-speed bicycle and many years older than his picture—a stark, somewhat cheesy black-and-white shot of a man in a tux with jet-black hair leaning on his portable keyboard. In person he was nowhere near as high contrast, but had more of a brownish, blended quality. He was not unattractive, though. I like nebbishy Jewish guys and they seem to like me.

He got us a latte (me) and an espresso (him) while I sat at a side-walk table in the mist. "Nice legs," said two guys walking by.

"When I saw you I was thinking 'It'd be nice if that were her.'" he said when he came out with our coffees and sat down. After we had our drinks, he and his bicycle walked me home and I found I liked him much more than I had anticipated.

Soon after, he got work playing the piano and singing on a cruise ship that took him from Alaska to the Panama Canal for

17

the rest of the summer. His act consisted of performing standards by people like Johnny Mathis and Cole Porter. Although he called fairly often to tell funny stories about his octogenarian groupies or the time his Books on Tape of the Bible melted from being left on a radiator ("it's now the Book of RooOOOwrooooth"), we hadn't seen each other since that morning at the coffee shop.

Now it was fall. He was back in town and wanted to take me to Sunday brunch. It was only our second date, so I still didn't know him well. Apparently he was on the fast track to change that. He told me about his romantic history as we waited on the restaurant's shallow steps and I quickly realized I was in too deep. He had moved from New York to Seattle to be with a woman to whom he was engaged but didn't seem to have known for long. Then there was Trudy, Annette, two Carolines . . . the guy has had more aborted engagements than Johnny Depp. By the time our table was ready he was already looking at me like I would be next.

Some women find being rushed by a guy early on to be flattering, but I never understand insta-macy or telling all in very early dating. I mean, where's the fire? Our conversation was thankfully interrupted by great Denver omelets and scones, which were really coffee cake with raspberry jam.

Since nothing says "I don't live in L.A. anymore" like crimson leaves and hot apple cider from roadside stands, I wanted to take a drive to the country to get a pumpkin for Halloween.

Glitter Ball told me that his father was a musician in the '60s. It became clear that his biggest artistic achievement was the people he hung out with. While my childhood memories are of a series of gray cats and my parents' martini-swilling friends, Glitter Ball's are of Bob Dylan, George Harrison, and John Lennon.

"I remember meeting John in a studio in Manhattan. He was abrupt. He was in the middle of recording and it wasn't going well," he said. "George was wonderful, though. He used to come to our house for Sunday dinner. He was so good to our family. He was just a nice man."

I've been to Liverpool twice. I've seen the red gate and shock of green grass at Strawberry Fields, Paul's boyhood home and John's boyhood home, Penny Lane and Eleanor Rigby's grave. But to actually have known them, especially John, well, I was beyond impressed.

"Would you mind if I wrote about you knowing the Beatles?" I said.

He took my hand as we got on the freeway. "It's yours."

Two degrees away from the Beatles. Could their rarefied sensibilities, their class and exquisite sense of grace, have influenced Glitter Ball as a child and as a young man? I decided they must have. How could they not? I leaned my head back against the seat of his truck and the autumn countryside showed off its gold and ruby as if it were a bracelet.

A handmade sign pointed us to the "Pumpkin Patch and Corn Maize." Passengers on a plane flying overhead would be able to see that the cornfield was mowed into animal shapes. Those of us on the ground could tell which animals we were in by little signs that gave us fun facts about them. In the rooster's beak, Glitter Ball suddenly pulled me to him and kissed me. He did it again in the sheep's nose and more fervently in the cow's udder.

By the time we were in the horse's ass I started to feel like I was in a different maze—the one from *The Shining*. Like Jack Nicholson being taken over by an evil, snowed-in hotel, Glitter Ball was taken over by his penis. There was something wrong and perverse about him sprouting horns in what was meant to be a family-oriented place. Small children ran by, horrified. "I'll show you some facts about animals," his penis seemed to say.

His kisses, requests, and expectations got harder and faster. He begged me to come for Christmas in New York, where he would be performing the lounge version of *The Nutcracker* at some of the finest hotels in Brooklyn. Visions of sugarplums mercifully showing me an escape route from this godforsaken cornfield danced in my head.

At least I got the answer to my question "Where's the fire?" It was crackling and roaring in Glitter Ball's pants. I realized it had been his penis telling me about all the broken engagements—hell, it was probably his penis that caused the engagements in the first place. It had taken me to brunch and now it was pressed against me in a cornfield.

Has there ever been an organ that is as credited with supernatural powers? In India it is viewed as sacred and allowed to wander the streets unattended. Or maybe that's cows. Or cats in Egypt. In any event, the penis is used as a catchall explanation by men for any number of bad behaviors and is conveniently the one excuse women cannot really prove is a lie. Not firsthand anyway. While the vagina just innocuously sits there in a sort of shrug with its hands open as if to say, "I don't know, whatever you want to do . . ." the penis is a divining rod for trouble: spending money its owner doesn't have, making promises he won't keep, and seeking out other women's innocuous shrugs.

What would the Beatles, who said "I'm happy just to dance with you," think of this? Maybe Glitter Ball hadn't been influenced by their rarefied sensibilities, class, and exquisite sense of grace after all.

When I finally staggered out of the cornfield, I was met by a cute goat in a pen, a real one this time. I took a picture of it. I picked out an oddly shaped $5 pumpkin, which Glitter Ball's penis insisted on paying for with a credit card, and we left at least one maze behind us.

On the way back, Glitter Ball talked about how his penis makes him unable to judge appropriately. Perhaps he thought I had been unconscious for the past three hours. Apart from that, the ride home was as silent as the gray October fog drifting in from the sound.

"I just want you to think about what it would be like to have a seven-inch clitoris," he finally said.

DATE 4 The Kind of Man I Should Want

TRUE CONFESSION

He seemed—for lack of a better phrase—so *grown-up* to me. Further proof that I am not quite ready to move on from the indiscretions of my youth, but instead look forward to seeing them again in the future.

The strangeness I was having with online dating made me decide that the next time I accepted a date it would be with someone I had already met. It seemed like a good idea to talk in person before committing myself to dinner and a cornfield.

I was downtown and it was 5:00 p.m., otherwise known as cocktail time, and since there's no better place to meet high-quality guys than in a bar while it's still daylight, I popped into a tony steakhouse. Young men in black bow ties jump to open the heavy doors; cranberry-colored cuts of meat are displayed in a glass case in the entryway. The restaurant is absolutely unaffordable to me, but the happy hour has beer-soaked prawns and tiny roast beef sandwiches with horseradish and mayo for $1.50. I love looking at the sleek women and men in suits from the nearby financial district. I love the solidity of the heavy wooden bar and the solvency implied by its cigar-smoking clientele.

Two men at the bar were waiting for a friend, but they gave up his seat for me.

"You three together?" said the bartender, all crisp white shirt and narrow black tie. He set cocktail napkins in front of us like he was dealing cards.

"No," I answered.

"She said that fast," the one in the suit who looked like Ed Harris said to the one in the brown bomber jacket who looked like John Goodman. "She didn't want to be associated with us for even a second."

They put my glass of white wine on their tab.

"Aren't you glad we dragged you out to happy hour? You work too much," John Goodman said to Ed Harris.

"This guy is here all the time," said Ed Harris about John Goodman.

It turned out that both men were working on a politically loaded urban project that didn't interest me in the slightest since it didn't affect me directly.

Topics that interest me radiate out from my mind like the rings from a stone tossed into a lake. Feng shui, Johnny Depp, and HBO are at the center. Mathematics, economic statistics, and technical explanations about anything lap at the very distant shore.

Ed Harris in the suit decided to pitch a conversational khaki tent on the sand by discussing big business's accounting practices, Nixon, and local Seattle politics. It made sense since he is an accountant who works with local politics.

Then again, John Goodman in the brown bomber jacket worked on the same project and his rock hit (*plop!*) right in the middle of my pleasure-seeking lake. He sat next to me and started talking about Napa. "Yeah, I love a good road trip," he said.

Napa. It would be harvest time there. The vines heavy with ripe fruit, the leaves turning gold against the dark, bluish gray sky. Four-poster beds in old Victorian homes, breakfasts of spiced turkey sausages and French toast laced through with thick cream custard and a side of hot maple syrup and berries. The flow of chardonnay and merlot and pinot noir.

Each man gave me his card.

I know perfectly well that when a woman meets two friends and they both give her their numbers that she is supposed to choose the one she likes best and call him. The one she chooses then immediately calls the one she didn't to say, "That woman we both met called me, we're going out Friday." I have seen this played out countless times with male friends, coworkers, and roommates. It's one of the things I love about men. If two women friends like the same man and he expresses an interest in both and then calls just one, the result is anything from a snorted, "You can have him," to catty remarks that circle back about three months later. Men know it's all a game, God bless them.

I did the unorthodox and called them both.

"Oh, Amy. Ed and I were just talking about you," said John Goodman. I had called Ed fifteen minutes before.

They both asked me out.

I walked down an alley in Pike Market and opened an unmarked pink door. The interior is decorated with pink lamps, mismatched floral tablecloths, and mismatched antique dishes. It is decidedly pink, but not queasily so, and is known for its drag-queen cabaret. We were to have drinks. Ed Harris was already sitting at a table waiting for me.

We ordered wine (me: the house pinot grigio, him: a merlot). He was planning on dinner. I wasn't, but rallied when I saw my half chicken limon with braised okra and sweet caramelized onions in a pastry shell. He gave me a nicely wrapped bottle of good chardonnay. It was a happy new dating trend maybe, the second time in two weeks that a man had given me a bottle of wine at dinner.

While we shared a caramel dessert with nuts and whipped cream (one plate, two spoons), he told me that he was divorced but that he had processed things and learned a lot. He said he was ready to get married again. I think divorced guys are a better bet than never-marrieds. They've committed, for a while at least.

Ed Harris is just a nice Seattle native. Polite, good job, good guy.

As we walked to his car, he explained that he had researched which kind would be most economical and how he had finally ended up buying his father's car because his father had also researched economical cars. It's a true testimony to my immaturity that I find talk of practicality and economy a total turnoff.

After dinner we decided to go for a drive in his used Toyota ("New cars lose a large percentage of their value the moment you drive them off the lot") and I suggested we go look at Halloween lights. We thought our best bet would be a funky, artsy, rapidly gentrifying neighborhood called Fremont. As we drove past houses with clever jack-o'-lanterns and orange twinkle lights and witches with accordion tissue-paper legs, Ed told me that his company had banned any sort of witch decorations in the break room or public areas because the three Wiccans in the graphic arts department found them an insult to real witches. The company retaliated somewhat by accusing one of the male Wiccans (so, warlock, I suppose) of dressing too "Goth," but the Wiccan countered by claiming religious discrimination and won. I would think a benefit of practicing witchcraft would be that you could circumvent regular corporate channels by casting spells and things, but that's probably discriminatory on my part too.

Ed was nervous saying good night and accidentally socked me in the jaw, something I suspect many, many men have thought to do and somehow restrained themselves from.

After I published the date on my Web site, I got the following e-mail from a married woman who claimed to be living vicariously through me (after she bitched about me not having enough dates up yet):

This is the guy you should be with. Look at what you said about him: *Ed Harris is just a nice Seattle native. Polite, good job, good guy.* That says it all. That's all you need.

Was it all I needed, though? Was I making this harder than it had to be? I reevaluated the date's highlights: Ed had made the joke "I really love music, but I'm not a musician; I play drums." I've heard it before, but it's still cute, I guess. I also enjoyed the story about the witches in the art department a lot. He also did some funny theater of the absurd at the restaurant, where he encouraged me to "Be a racehorse, because a squirrel on a racetrack just looks stupid!" and stormed off. Actually the last one was from a homeless guy I saw when I was on my way to the bathroom, but it still added to the evening.

Ed had told me that he was once so in love he got a speeding ticket. "We had just had a great date and I had the radio up loud, the windows open . . . I was so happy I didn't realize how fast I was going."

Surely this was the kind of guy I should be with. I wasn't feeling much chemistry but I did feel that I should develop a more mature taste in men. He was very sweet, reliable, called when he said he would, and wanted to get married again. He's the kind of guy that we women say we want, so when he asked me out for Halloween, I said yes.

BUNK DEBUNK

Myth: You can't meet anyone decent at a bar.

Debunked!

It may be more women than men who think this, but as the tequila-swilling bleached blonde who gave me my first job in L.A. used to say, "Sooner or later, everyone goes to a bar." (Often my "advisers" tend to be codependents, drunks, sex addicts . . . hey, even a stopped clock is right twice a day.)

Sure, if a bar stool actually has his name on it, you may not want to get involved—unless hanging out at that particular spot at least four nights a week is a social goal for you—but a few of my nicest (and hottest) friends have met their husbands at bars. Some of the most marriage-minded men I've dated (plus several favorites who weren't) were guys I met at bars, so I can personally recommend this method.

Now we're back to the stopped clock thing, aren't we . . .

DATE 5 The Kind of Man I Do Want

TRUE CONFESSION

He seemed grown-up to me, too, but more in the "Mommy and Daddy are going to watch a grown-up film now, so you have to go to bed" sort of way.

If Ed Harris was the guy I knew I should want, John Goodman was the man I wanted in spite of myself. One appealed to my head and the other appealed to someplace lower.

We were having drinks at the same pricey steakhouse where we met. He had been anticipating a nightmarish meeting earlier that day and explained that that was why he needed to meet me as early as possible (4:30) for a relaxing drink.

I was already predisposed to liking him the best of anyone I'd dated since I started the site. I told myself it was because he reminded me of John Goodman (as Dan Conner on *Roseanne*, and not the dangerous psycho from *Barton Fink*, obviously).

He was drinking a greyhound and smoking a cigar and wearing the brown leather jacket. I ordered a martini with lots of olives.

"If this contract doesn't come through, I don't know what I'm going to do next, but in a way it would be a relief. I'm a renegade. I don't like to be bound up by work every day. Big risks, big payoffs."

Yes, I thought. *That's for me.*

"Not sure I'd stay in Seattle, though," he continued. "I'm sick of needing my headlights on at three in the afternoon because it's so gloomy. So what kind of writing do you do?"

"First-person nonfiction," I said.

"Wow, that's great," he said. "I like narrative nonfiction. I'm reading *Confederates in the Attic*."

He told me about the book. So my Web site wasn't quite about a journalist who followed Civil War reenactment people around. It still wasn't a lie exactly. I felt too lightweight telling him I'm a dating writer. There was the feel of history about him, something old and earthy and rich, something that didn't have to do with the impermanence of the Internet. He told me about a woman friend of his. She was in New Orleans and it was about 3:00 a.m. She got arrested for public indecency with a young man—a really young man. It would probably have been okay except that they were on the courthouse steps. "You have to be pretty lewd to be considered lewd in New Orleans. It's one of the things I love about her," he said.

If asked to describe my physical type, I would probably come up with the archetype of the skinny British rock star or his wannabe Hollywood counterpart—a reedlike, tall body and a mop of straight hair with bangs—the kind of man who is boyish looking even into his fifties by sheer force of will.

The truth is that my reaction to John Goodman had nothing to do with my head or my pre–thought-out answer about what type of man I like. He was big, solid, not fat exactly, but not thin. My first boyfriend out of college had been built like a tennis player, lean, tall. We had broken up and he had left the state and gone home to his parents. I was destroyed. About six months later he came back and all those dinners of meat loaf and Betty Crocker brownies had transformed him from lean to fatty—not obese, not flabby, but definitely overweight. I didn't know if it was just that I was so relieved to be back together with him or that the swell of his lower belly now rose into my body like it was molded to me, but our sex life, always rabid, somehow miraculously got better. I've never viewed overweight men the same way since.

There is something about a man who will give himself over to food and drink that's infinitely sexier than the kind of man who counts calories or takes out a personal ad that says "I like to keep fit."

John Goodman was Bacchus—the wine, the weight, the pursuit of pleasure at the cost of cookie-cutter appearances. Ironically he didn't seem to be offering dinner. I was starving, so I asked, "Do you mind if I eat?"

"Get her whatever she wants, Ellie," he said to a middle-aged waitress with overprocessed blonde hair as he excused himself to go make a phone call.

I ordered and he came back. The bloody juices from my steak circled around the mound of garlic mashed potatoes while he told me stories of his travels for the better part of an hour.

"I have to go feed my kids," he said after my leftovers were boxed up and his second greyhound was drained. "Come on, I'll give you a ride home." I was disappointed. It was still early. I wondered if he was really divorced like he had said. "We'll have to go to a Cajun place I know of next time," he said. "Their food's like a four-alarm fire. You'll love it."

When I hugged him good-bye, he felt solid but his brown leather jacket was like butter to my hands.

DATE 6 Mismatched Costumes on Halloween

TRUE CONFESSION

I love haunted houses, vampires, witches, and ghosts; I'm just not sure they're great additions to a date night.

I was regretting that I had agreed to dress in costume for Halloween. I had a date with Ed Harris but it wasn't like we were even going to a party. The plan was to have dinner and then walk around and look at costumes. We would just be this lone straight couple wandering around the main drag of the predominantly gay part of town. If I changed my mind, Ed would have accommodated me. He was that kind of guy. I decided to be a good sport about it.

Normally Halloween is my favorite holiday, because it's not tied to family angst or spending a lot of money on other people, but this year I was in a funk. I had been doing freelance work for my former company, a big online entertainment guide. My latest project was reviewing restaurants, which for any other employer is probably lots of fun. I'm always reading food reviews that paint a picture of good friends sharing daring entrées and pithy conversation. My employer wouldn't pay for meals though, so at each restaurant I had to ask if I could sit down alone and just have water while I reviewed the décor and guessed at what the food might taste like if I worked for someone who would pay for it. The restaurants were assigned by type, so one week I sat and had water at a dozen Japanese restaurants; the next, at a dozen diners. That week I was sipping *agua* at Mexican places and feeling a renewed sense of frustration at not having my own newspaper column. My own Web site, on the other hand, was doing fantastically. I had readers in thirty-five countries and had made almost $100 in donations from fans.

My costume was Madonna from the "Material Girl" video. I wore a pink satin strapless gown, lots of rhinestones, and blonde in my hair. Since that video is a takeoff on Marilyn Monroe, I guess I was really dressing as her. I had originally considered going as Marilyn, but knew that tons of men would be dressed as her, and it's always so embarrassing to have a guy with better legs show up in the same outfit.

Ed Harris went as Abraham Lincoln. We were mismatched.

As his Toyota climbed the steep slope to Broadway, he asked me about my week. I told him that I was bored to death with the freelance work and wanted my own column.

"What sort of a column would you like to write?"

"One about dating, relationships, you know, but funny."

"I only read political columns," he said as if that were the end of it. "A lot of people would feel lucky to be a professional writer at all, you know."

I weakly replied that unpublished kids just getting out of school might be happy with the work I'd been doing, but I was not. There I was, the Material Girl and her immaterial concerns. It made me remember why I usually date other artists: instead of a dismissive comment, the whole evening's conversation would have been an empathy fest about how hard it is to get recognition for our brilliant creative work and how wrong the rest of the world is to not acknowledge us.

Dismissing my artistic misery is one of my deal breakers. Some women consider smoking, drinking, or children deal breakers. They are likely to look at things like a man's income or education. Clearly those women have no imagination.

I look at what films a man has seen, his views on Beatles music, and which specific countries he has traveled to. Deal breakers for me would include most Bruce Willis movies, only liking "Got to Get You Into My Life," and considering Canada exotic. I also carefully observe how a man views my writing.

Unbeknownst to him, a man who dates me is in a delicate situation where even the most seemingly innocent comment could be a relationship-ending land mine. "I only read *political* columns." *Bang!* "You're lucky you even get to be a writer, lots of people would trade places with you." *Boom!* "I saw a silent film recently and realized how meaningless words are." *Kablooey!*

We had dinner at one of the better Thai restaurants I've been to. There we shared a bottle of hot sake and some beef dish with peppers, mushrooms, and onions and a sweet, spicy chicken panang with peanut sauce, coconut milk, and slivers of peppers that I had seen mentioned by a restaurant critic who was apparently allowed to order food to write about.

After dinner Ed Harris and I walked down the street and looked at people and their costumes. It was my first time seeing Halloween in Seattle and Ed had said it was a really wild spectacle, but once again I was disappointed in his assessment of things. In Los Angeles the Halloween "parade" is a street party of ten thousand people and attracts costumes fit for the movies and in some cases lifted from their wardrobe departments.

People in Seattle had a much folksier interpretation of October 31. Small groups clustered around in the below-freezing night air. Huddled together smoking with their brightly colored costumes peeking out from under their overcoats, they resembled refugee burnouts from a high school play.

As if to reflect my mood, a group of people dressed in black walked by carrying a coffin. It had the words Our Civil Rights painted on it in white, but I'm not sure they were even in costume.

I was freezing and I knew this wasn't going anywhere. Ed Harris had crossed the line between being mature to being patronizing with his writing comment. It was time to go.

I didn't laugh at his jokes on the way home. It wasn't on purpose, I truly didn't get them. I did purposely answer, "The younger men here," when he asked me what I like best about Seattle, though. He's in his forties.

Outside of the Hendrix museum we saw a group of guys elaborately and accurately dressed as a full Catholic processional, complete with a cardinal. It was a group costume fit for Los Angeles. Ed thought they were druids.

He asked me to a movie and I told him to just call me later in the week. I didn't want to agree to anything right then since I knew I didn't want to see him again. He called like he said he would and I never called him back.

Just as reliably, John Goodman also called, apologized for not calling in a while, made vague promises about getting together soon, then never called again. So far John Goodman had been my favorite of the guys I had dated, and, while I wasn't positive he was still married, it did seem suspicious that he had to be home by 6:00 p.m.

The next week I was having drinks with a girl friend and I realized over $10 house merlots and Dungeness-crab-and-corn chowder that I like unavailable men.

It's like that movie The Tao of Steve, where the overweight slacker was scoring with every chick in town. He attributed his success with women to his philosophy: be disinterested (women can smell it if you *really* want them), be excellent (do something great in her presence), be gone (disappear and she will seek you out). This really does work in real life. Or maybe I just have the romantic maturity of a fourteen-year-old.

I saw my grocery store crush and he told me that he had ended up working on Halloween night. "Two girls came in wearing body paint and nothing else. After about forty-five minutes I had to ask them to leave."

"What are you doing for Thanksgiving?" I asked, partly to try to sniff out whether or not he had a girlfriend. "Going to my grandma's, I do every year," he said.

Good! No involvement that I could tell anyway. He seemed to be just right for me, with the naughty comment about Halloween, which indicated a healthy sex drive, and the sweet plans to go to Grandma's for Thanksgiving (just like in the song), which indicated homeyness and stability. I felt slightly and absurdly let down that he didn't ask me to do anything on Thanksgiving since I didn't have any plans. I wouldn't have had to come along to his grandmother's but dessert and wine after dinner would have at least been something to look forward to.

As it was I cooked a turkey breast for myself with cranberries and pumpkin pie and rented *GoodFellas*. I had never seen it before. It was great.

BUNK DEBUNK

Myth: *Women are attracted to unavailable men.*

Bunked!

It's not that I think most women have a deep-seated need to re-create the abandonment from their childhoods in an attempt to resolve the issue as adults, it's that I'm a firm believer in social Darwinism. I think that men with the most to offer naturally have more women interested in them, so are less eager to cut off their options by settling down.

DATE 7 The First-Date Breakup

TRUE CONFESSION

I had a big argument with several girl friends about the relative hideousness of being formally dumped after only one date, with half feeling that it was very considerate to keep a woman from waiting by the phone in a taking-the-traditional-masculine-role sort of way and the other half of us feeling that it's sickeningly presumptuous and that we wouldn't have seen the losers again even if they had called for a second date.

There's something old-fashioned and human about the personals in the back of the free weekly paper that comes out on Thursdays. Since they don't include pictures, there is not the rapid-fire dismissal of the physically less fortunate that takes place with online dating. One can get a sense of the ad placer's inner self, hopes, and fears, insofar as twenty-five words or less will allow, anyway. A phone message box is also in place so you can get a real feel for the other person through their voice, something the e-mail–based online matchmaking services don't provide. I will never fully recover from the time I met a British doctor from Match.com who turned out to be a nurse from Milwaukee, something I would have known had we spoken first.

Since I didn't have time to place an ad of my own, I skimmed the *Seattle Weekly*. "SWM, 40, 6', 175. Thoughtful, published writer with a love of Italy seeks passionate, intelligent woman 35–45 for

DINK lifestyle. Race open." He sounded perfect for me. I didn't know much about this DINK lifestyle, but I'll pretty much try anything if I'm attracted to someone and have had enough wine.

We talked on the phone and he sounded great—sophisticated and fun. We met for dinner at an Italian bistro and he brought me a slender long-stemmed red rose.

He reminded me of Rick Steves, the local tourist-guide writer who has a show on the Travel Channel, but then lots of Washington guys do with their wire-rimmed glasses and short hair and pleasant smiles.

He told me he had written a science fiction book and had lived in an Italian monastery. He knew just how to order. He was decisive. He had risotto with asparagus and shrimp (was too bland for him), I had tiny veal ravioli with marinara sauce (was just okay) and we split a bottle of Orvieto, which is a dry white wine from an Italian town he's been to. We were the only people in the quiet back room.

He told me I looked like the woman who replaced Shelley Long on *Cheers*. He asked me why I had my hands in my lap and said that they were so beautiful they should be shown. He engaged me with conversation that had nothing to do with his problems, neuroses, or hang-ups about "ex" women in his life. He seemed really great. I was surprised that he was still single. "You seem really great. Is there a reason you're still single?" I asked.

"Yes," he said. "I don't want kids and most of the women I meet do."

"You seem like you'd be a cool dad, though," I said.

"I'm the oldest of a big family and I looked after my younger siblings a lot . . . too much, really. I feel like I've been there, done that, and I don't want to go through raising kids of my own."

We closed the place. He ran back to the restaurant for me when I forgot my doggie box and he walked me home. It was a great date.

The next day I called one of my girl friends and found out that "DINK lifestyle" wasn't a typo for a free-for-all of constant sexual readiness, but was instead an acronym for "Double Income, No Kids."

Although he was wonderful, I couldn't imagine a life with such an extraordinary option cut off from me completely. Was there no room for discussion about it? Not even if I turned out to be the right woman for him and we felt that something was missing from our lives? It's the deepest expression of commitment between a man and a woman. Everyone from my own parents to A-list movie stars says it's shown them a capacity for love they didn't know existed before.

What kind of a man would deny me at least the option of not working?

As it turned out, I needn't have worried. A week later he called me to tell me he wasn't going to be calling. He assured me that it didn't take away from our night together, but that there was someone else. He was going to keep my number, but he didn't expect me to wait for him. Soldiers leaving their high school sweethearts to go off to fight World War II were less dramatic. Why couldn't he just have disappeared like a normal guy? I don't need to be told, "It's not you, it's me," after one date.

I found out more about what was behind the first-date breakup when I attended a party at a new club called Heaven. It was being thrown by my girl friend Anastasia.

I had just gotten in line to get a drink when I met a man. He was immaculate: jet-black hair, pale blue eyes, tall, and clean looking. He asked if I was single and said he was too. Our conversation immediately turned to dating experiences.

"I do Match.com, eHarmony, speed dating, and social clubs," he said.

"I've never done speed dating," I said.

"Oh, you should, if only for the experience. You meet between seven and twenty people in an evening for three to ten minutes each. You get a tally sheet and can check off who you want to see again."

"And how many women do you usually check off?"

"One . . . every other time I do it."

"That's not many."

"I'm picky. I date over thirty women a month, but I'm only interested in one percent of them."

He continued. "I think dating needs to be kinder; it can be so fraught with rejection and heartbreak. So I e-mail or call all the women I don't pick to tell them that I won't be seeing them again, and to thank them for the conversation and to wish them luck."

"So you contact the other ninety-nine percent that you don't want to see?"

"Yeah, it takes a long time, but I think it's worth it to create a positive feeling in the dating world."

"Having a guy completely vanish off the face of the earth if he doesn't want an undying commitment with me creates a positive feeling in my dating world. That way I can tell myself he just got hit by a car or something and not that he wasn't attracted to me. I don't need the humiliation of being broken up with after one date."

He then went on to tell me that he had met not one, but two women he considered prime candidates in the past month, so I knew I was statistically out of the running. I felt he was wasting my time. There was a whole room of bachelors who didn't have such high standards. Surely one of them could be buying me my next drink while pretending not to stare at my cleavage.

Later I ran into Anastasia. "I just met a guy who told me he dates over one hundred women a quarter," I said.

"No," Anastasia said.

"He's including speed dating and online dating and It's Just

Lunch, but, yes, he does. He likes one out of one hundred and he e-mails or calls the other ninety-nine to tell them he's not going to be calling again. He dates over four hundred women a year. That's more than one woman a day."

"No, he can't."

"Yep. I wish there were a way to immediately extract yourself from a conversation with a man the instant you realize things aren't going to work. I mean, when he said that he's only interested in one in one hundred and he'd already met two this month, I knew my odds weren't good. I wish there were like a cosmic buzzer that went off when you realized that things weren't going anywhere."

"Like a cross between a message from God and *The Gong Show*," said Anastasia.

"There's the guy I was talking about," I said, nodding toward him.

"Oh, I know him," said Anastasia. "He has OCD—obsessive compulsive disorder."

I might have known that a guy who wants to leave women with a positive feeling after he rejects them has a disorder.

When I got home I looked up OCD and according to the Mayo Clinic it's technically a mental illness. Maybe that DINK guy who broke up with me after our first date at the Italian place was mentally ill.

Then I realized that the immaculate man had indeed left me with a positive feeling about the dating world: maybe *all* the guys who don't want to continue seeing me are mentally ill.

DATE 8 Picked Up a Guy Walking Down the Street

TRUE CONFESSION

I felt light-years away from my days on Match.com, which were in reality only five dates ago. Getting asked out in the course of my normal day makes me feel like Julia Roberts doing a "meet cute" scene in a romantic comedy.

Here are some ways to get dates, in order of difficulty:

- With **online dating**, you're basically taking cautious baby steps to the door of the plane from which you are about to jump. Lulled and misled by the seeming safety of e-mail, you will be tempted to send an airbrushed picture of yourself taken ten years ago, lie about your age, weight, and athletic skills, and grossly inflate your income. Yes, the "online" part is easy enough; it's being thrown into the unflattering fluorescent light of the actual dating that's horrifying. Not to worry. If you've showed any restraint at all and lied only slightly less than the total stranger you are about to meet, you're the winner!

- **Fix-ups** can be incredibly good or perfectly awful, but they always, always say more about your relationship to the fixer-upper than they do about anything else. You can definitely tell exactly what your friends think of you by who they think is "perfect for you."

A woman I worked with once wanted to set me up with her cousin. "He really, really needs to be with someone. He's so lonely and desperate," she said. "Can I pencil you in for Friday?"

• **Singles "networking" clubs** are great, as the ugly question of whether or not someone is available is removed. There is at least the illusion that everyone there is just yours for the taking. Oh, except those misguided souls who actually believed the "networking" part. Be careful which club you affiliate yourself with, though, as some are very *Love Boat*–gone-bad.

• The **errands-and-street-traffic method** is the most advanced way of getting a date, but it is also the most fulfilling, because you sound cool when you're telling friends about it later. It's free and you can do it anywhere, since it is basically just getting a date as you go about your normal business—buying tomatoes or hinges or making a coffee run to Starbucks. The hard part is that alcohol and nightclub lighting are rarely involved. On the plus side, married people are off guard and less likely to waste your time by not wearing their wedding rings. A complex system of coy eye contact, totally made-up excuses to talk, and feigned interest in what the other person has to say works best in this scenario.

Actually, I guess it's like every other kind of dating.

Like a contestant correctly answering questions on a game show, I was getting dates with a higher and higher level of difficulty. My success online led to my success at a bar, which brought me to the most advanced skill level of all: getting a date by just walking down the street. It's the kind of thing that always happens on television and in the movies, but beyond the age of twenty-five, really how common is it to meet a normal man in the frozen-food aisle or at Blockbuster? Desperation to not fall on my face with the Web site had whipped me into peak shape.

I first met him in the wine aisle of a discount gourmet grocery store. He was a big, cuddly, bearish man with thick graying hair and an incongruously soft voice. He had an East Coast accent that I loved.

"I always see you at the health food place," he said.

I knew it definitely wasn't me because I don't like health food when it's labeled as such. It's trying too hard for one thing. I think because fewer people shop at those stores the nuts and juices are less fresh than at the regular unhealthy food store. I did not say any of this to him, though, because I have learned as a burgeoning dating expert that men don't necessarily need a factual rundown of how mistaken and wrong they are when we first meet. There is plenty of time for that after we're involved.

"Don't you love their sandwiches?" he continued.

Jesus, I don't even eat their dried cranberries and there's not much that can go wrong with those. I would never trust them with a sandwich. I don't even remember seeing a refrigerator there.

"No, I haven't tried them!" I said brightly.

I added a $3 bottle of chardonnay and some fully refrigerated hummus to my red plastic basket and got in line behind him at the checkout. I felt cocky and attractive. I was sure that as he reached into his wallet he was going to give me his card. Instead he pulled out some money and paid the cashier.

A week later I completely surprised myself by buying a turkey sandwich at the health food store he had mentioned. As I predicted, it was dry and may or may not have been refrigerated. When I was walking out, I ran into him. "I told you I see you here," he said. "I work for a local magazine in this neighborhood."

"I'm a writer."

"Here's my card, send me some samples. We'll have lunch." Boom. Four sentences. That's how it's done when you're skilled.

Unrefrigerated Sandwich Recommender said he'd get back to me about my writing and then didn't, but he did make good on the date invite. We met up at the ubiquitous health food store, where a blonde woman was handing out samples of powdered protein eggnog that was as bad as it sounds. She told us it tastes better if you add brandy, but what doesn't?

He and I walked to a cute Chinese place around the corner.

We got a nice booth and over egg rolls and hot-and-sour soup and spicy chicken and vegetables in brown garlic sauce (lunch specials, both) we talked about our views on Seattle and other cities we've lived in (him: San Francisco, New York, and Jackson Hole, Wyoming; me: Minneapolis and L.A.).

"I could tell right away you weren't from here," he said. "You seemed so approachable." Seattle has a terrible reputation for being closed to outsiders, which includes anyone not born here. "Have you found it very easy to make friends?" he asked.

"No, I've found it difficult. I don't have many friends, especially with not working."

I didn't mention that I thought it was easy to get dates, though. More and more I was feeling dragged down by not having anything but dating for a social life. Christmastime was making it worse.

"Maybe we can be friends," he said.

"That sounds good," I said, and meant it.

We discovered we both had birthdays coming up. He was a much better representative of the legendary Sagittarian joie de vivre and love of travel than I, though. He talked of going to a bed and breakfast by himself, reading a great book and eating marionberry pie at a diner, then hiring a guide to take him salmon fishing.

"I threw all the fish back, though. I felt bad for them."

"I would do the same."

He is a gentle giant. A lover of animals (well, of fish anyway) and of music.

He is a concert addict and saw Paul McCartney here. "The

show opened with twenty minutes of Indian dancing. I thought I was either at the wrong concert or it was supposed to be a representation of the Beatles' drug phase."

Our lunch lasted two hours and he said he felt unmotivated to work because it was such a gray Monday. I pretended to be unable to grasp the concept of feeling unambitious, but of course knew that I would go home and do nothing for the rest of the day.

I opened my fortune cookie. "It is good to know that things are improving," it read.

BUNK DEBUNK

Myth: *The more men you already have, the more you attract.*

Bunked!

Maybe it's because the pathetic stink of desperation is off you. Maybe it's because people just want what everyone else wants. Maybe it's that, as one of my friends argues, when you're having sex all the time it releases pheromones, the smell that attracts mates (granted, she's a sex addict and will use anything to justify it, but she may still be onto something).

In any event, I see time and time again that it's easier to attract people when you're (1) already involved, (2) already having bunches-o'-sex, or (3) already married, which, although it shows you're not afraid to commit, is just a bad situation for everyone if you really think about it.

DATE 9 Getting Some Trim

TRUE CONFESSION

The traditional definition of a date is that it includes both food and entertainment. I wanted this to be one so badly that I put on a CD and ate pasta and tomato-basil sauce while the guy was setting up my Christmas tree.

I found out that my crush from the grocery store is not as young as he looks (and, to be fair, acts), but, rather, is thirty-three. I also found out that he is the manager and not just a bag boy. I mentally replaced the fantasy of myself as a bored, sophisticated-yet-horny housewife who is drawn into a crazy, wild sexual affair with a stock boy who has more muscles than brains, which plays out late at night in the dairy section (with its endless possibilities involving custard-style yogurt, nondairy whipped cream, etc.), with the fantasy of a crazy, wild sexual affair between equals (providing one of the equals is an overeducated writer and the other, well, let's be honest, still has more muscles than brains but has street smarts and is very sweet and is at least not embarrassingly younger) which happens behind the locked door of his office. Much more respectable, since the newer scenario doesn't involve adultery, it is in the afternoon instead of after closing, and although I show up at the store needing to speak to the manager wearing nothing but a raincoat, it is Seattle, so at least the raincoat itself is not as gratuitous as it would be in some place like Phoenix.

One of the first things I noticed when I moved to Seattle was how nice the waiters, coffee shop people, and drugstore people are compared to those in Los Angeles, where it was always implied that better, more exciting customers had been there just before you and would soon be again.

In Seattle: ask a question about the nearest place to kayak and the coffee counter magically closes behind you so the barista can talk about Lake Union. Drag yourself out of the rain and into a pizza place looking like a wet cat and the waiter immediately removes your soaking coat from your arms. I once asked directions of the man who owns the Korean market on the corner and he closed shop for fifteen minutes so he could walk me there.

It's wonderful, of course, but it's confusing if you're attracted to someone who works in the service industry. The guy from the grocery store had been on my radar and in my consciousness for months, but it wasn't until I mentioned that I needed a Christmas tree for my apartment and he offered to help me get one that I realized he might be more than just a good customer service provider.

I was so excited all week. I was finally going out with my big crush. Not a date exactly, but maybe we would go for dinner afterward.

I met him at the store and he was ready to go. He swept me out the door and into his truck. His cell phone immediately began ringing off the hook. Someone wants to get ahold of him bad, I thought as he looked at the display and shut it off.

It was of course pouring rain and we got really lost and saw so many beautiful twinkle lights and decorations on houses in the neighborhoods we accidentally wound our way through. "Have you ever been golfing?" he asked as we passed a nine-hole course.

"Yes, it was hard!"

"I've been once and I didn't like it. I got frustrated," he said. "I only like things I don't have to work for."

He had called ahead and scouted out several places that had

trees. I felt taken care of, but was a little surprised that he had never been to Ballard, the neighborhood where the lot was located. It was close by and he had worked in Seattle for years. Maybe that's what I needed though, some guy who was content to be where he already was and not continually searching. Maybe this was the Seattle me: dating a simple, homey, athletic type instead of some Hollywood hipster musician.

He was one of the only people I considered even a casual friend. I was attracted to his gapped teeth and rough and tumble empathy. I liked him. He would ask me twenty questions about myself every time I saw him and remember my answers weeks later. He had dark blue eyes and was not overly handsome, so would likely be faithful. I had a crush on him.

"I like that one," he said immediately. "It's not mechanically cut and it has a good shape, but it has a hole near the top. That's probably why it's left. I like it when they have flaws." He smiled at me.

"Do you need help carrying it?" I called up the stairs to my third-floor apartment as I followed behind him.

"Uh, no." He laughed. I guess it wasn't heavy to him. He did look strong.

I've always thought of the Christmas tree guy as a nice person, but sort of too Dudley Do-Right for me. He seemed to take on more personality once we were in my apartment, though. His sense of humor was dry and he had a great appreciation for the hardwood floors and crown molding of my '20s apartment, even though he is not gay.

I put on Django Reinhardt, a guitarist from the '30s whose music was featured in the great Woody Allen movie *Sweet and Lowdown*. It was kind of weird music to put on with a guy over and as I expected, Christmas Tree had never heard of him. He didn't want food or wine, while I had both, so I was not sure it was a date, although I counted it toward the fifty on my Web site the next day.

He started to set up the tree and said something about team-work. I couldn't hear him as I was in the kitchen pouring myself a glass of wine and eating ravioli. I helped him by standing around and saying things like "That doesn't look straight."

My heart was warmed by his sweet comment about teamwork, though. He was a simple guy, really an all-American. Maybe I could be the dark complex one in the relationship and he would supply the stability and the sincerity. Sure he didn't have a lot of money, I bet, but he seemed responsible and it's supposed to be more important to save than to make a lot.

He told me his dad had spent all Sunday with him showing him how to fix his car.

"Now I'll be able to teach my own son someday," he said. "I have eight sisters and I'm my dad's only son."

As soon as the tree was set up, he said he had to do some Christmas shopping at Bed Bath & Beyond before it closed. With eight sisters I'd guess he'd probably be there all the time.

I've heard that the true litmus test of how you feel about some-one is if you genuinely enjoy doing mundane errands with them. Is it fun buying oranges or toothpaste or lug nuts together? Is wait-ing in the grocery line an annoying drag or do you kiss and imag-ine weird dialogue that the other patrons may be saying? Are you one of those tag-team couples who has one person wait while the other still shops and then at the last minute shoves a huge cart with eighty-seven items in front of the poor single person with three? I hate that.

I had definitely had a great time. But buying a Christmas tree with him hadn't felt like a mundane errand . . . it had felt like magic.

DATE 10 But He Was So Good on Paper . . .

TRUE CONFESSION

Tonight I got the answer to the question: When is having an outstanding résumé—both personally and professionally—and looking like JFK Jr. meaningless?

"She's had sixteen abortions, you know. Her personal trainer was on the show and he told us all about it." The host of *Good Day, Seattle!*, a local talk show on which I was appearing, was referring to one of the biggest pop stars in the world. I was shocked. Not by the abortions exactly, but by the fact that one of her employees would dish the dirt that way. I would never say that kind of thing about a boss to someone in the media. You would think that discretion would be a valued trait in a celebrity personal trainer . . . and to think I can't find a job. Now the host was making the same mistake by retelling the story in front of me, a well-known blabbermouth. The very reason I was on her show was lack of discretion about my love life, after all. Ironic. I didn't believe the abortion story anyway. Not because I thought the pop star was too pure to have abortions, but because she is a well-known control freak and it seemed out of character for her to have such a loose grip on something as simple as preventing pregnancy. Surely she would have caught on that the Pill is less trouble after the ninth or tenth round.

I was waiting in a special area of the lobby reserved for guests of the show. I watched as the audience members were all frisked and made to walk through a metal detector. You would think since the topic of the program was Crazy Web Sites and the People Who Start Them that I would be the one getting frisked, but no.

I had been recommended to the producer by Penny, a woman with a popular Web site called Help Me Leave My Husband, after she and I had bonded over how to deal with rude e-mails from people. I had already had my fill of cruelty from strangers just for going on dates. Since she was asking for people to send money so she could divorce her husband who was overseas defending our country, she had attained mentorlike status to me.

Penny had been on TV several times before and the only advice she had for me was not to wear ugly boots, so I picked out a cute black pair that came to my knees. Since I didn't have many dress clothes that were right for Seattle, I wore a black fitted jacket and black pants that are above the ankle. They are meant to be worn with strappy sandals, but they would blend with the black boots. They were a little too tight, but you wouldn't be able to tell on TV.

It was live television, so it was very exciting and fast paced. There was a man with a headset just off camera giving cues like an air traffic controller the whole time.

My portion of the interview included:

Host: Do the men you write about know you're writing about them?

Me: Not always. I'd like to keep it a secret. You know, so the project seems more authentic.

Host: You want to keep it a secret? You're on television, Amy. What if you fall in love?

Me: I'm sure anyone who really loves me will also love my Web site.

It had gone well. I had said everything I had to say about my dates. It wasn't too much or too little and now I could just relax.

The last fifteen minutes of the show was going to be phone calls from people with crazy Web sites in other parts of the country. We had a commercial break and Penny had barely finished her suggestion that they start keeping a big bottle of Vicodin in the greenroom when the air traffic controller man said to the host, "The phone lines are down, so the rest of the show is scrapped. And we're live in five, four, three . . ."

"Tell us more about your Web site, Amy," she said.

Afterward we watched the footage of the show and I had a horrifying flash of recognition: with the tight, short pants and black boots I looked like Captain Kirk from the waist down. And when I was talking, the camera kept cutting back and forth between me and a pretty blonde college girl who was about nineteen, the implication clearly being that it was she who should have a dating project and, oh God, "love me, love my Web site."

For the next two weeks I got e-mails saying things like: "I think I love you, but is it okay if your Web site and I are just friends?" "Who was that really attractive blonde?" and "Beam me up, Scotty."

A few nights later I had another live appearance, this time one-on-one: I had a blind date from Match.com.

His lanky, easy manner and good looks recalled prep schools in New England and financial windfalls in Palo Alto. He and his college roommate had started an online music company that was snapped up by RealNetworks in the late '90s. He took that money and started a program to educate underprivileged children, a project he also writes a thoughtful newspaper column about. I don't read Harlequin romances, but if they were set in twenty-first-century Seattle, he would be on the cover with his shirt unbuttoned and his loins straining. He was perfect on paper.

Unfortunately our date was in 3-D and not paperback. We sat down and just looked at each other for an uncomfortable eternity—it felt like ten seconds, but it may have been even longer.

He had suggested a beautiful Mexican place and we got a booth in back, although we would have had our choice—we were the only ones there. It was a restaurant that had dancing later, but we were so early that the fountain in the middle of the room wasn't even turned on yet. Red and green and silver tinsel was strung across the balcony above us. It was Christmastime.

Our lack of chemistry was palpable and I was sure it was mutual. In a sort of unspoken "I will if you will," we committed to spending the next hour together by ordering dinner. I had chicken enchiladas with *salsa verde* and rice and beans. He had chile rellenos and about two bowls of chips with the perfectly spiced salsa.

He asked me how my week had been. I didn't want to tell him about the talk show, because I didn't want to tell him that I'd be writing about our date, so it left me with little to say.

Part of the reason for my reticence was that for one thing I hadn't yet decided how I was going to handle telling men I was writing about them on an increasingly public forum, but with this man in particular, I felt a little ashamed. Not only had he been a more successful dot-commer and writer than I am, but with his program to help underprivileged children, he just seemed to be a better person.

I didn't want to tell him about any of this, so when he asked how my week had been, I just answered, "Fine."

He kept lingering after dinner, and I finally suggested we go.

We walked toward our houses (it was a long way) and when we got to a high-rise overlooking the water he said, "Well, this is me," rather than seeing me home. I said, "Have a nice Christmas," and didn't even stop walking, just sort of said it over my shoulder. There was not even a token "We should get together" or insincere "I'll call you" from him.

Then I realized I had left my purse at the restaurant and had to walk all the way back to get it by myself.

The next day he e-mailed me to wish me luck with my writing

and to tell me there was no chemistry between us. Did he truly think after *that* date it needed to be said?

What sort of a man lets a woman walk home alone at night, though? Technically it was me who saw him safely home. Maybe I was being too hard on myself before. Maybe it was I who was the better person.

It was my birthday. In five days it would be Christmas. It was with mixed feelings and many more e-mails including no less than three referencing Klingons that I found out that ABC News had picked up what I was now thinking of as the *Star Trek* interview. Why did everything in my life have to have a catch? I got on television and came off like an idiot, I met someone perfect on paper and probably would have had more chemistry with Mr. Spock, I finally got to go out with Christmas Tree and we were no closer to dating than we were last fall.

I found out later that the pop star kept secrets about as well as I do. Not only was she unashamed of her abortions, she had interviewed about them in a cover story for *Spin*.

It must be that the sociobiologists really have it right. It's all about procreation. That we're attracted to those who have compatible immune systems and that we can recognize each other by our smell. Maybe that's why the pop star keeps getting pregnant. Maybe that's why I want to be with Christmas Tree, who says things like "hotty toddy" instead of "hot toddy" (and it's not because he's trying to be cute, it's because he is unable to recognize any alcoholic drink more sophisticated than beer). He does smell good, though.

BUNK DEBUNK

Myth: Online dating is perfect because you can just use a checklist to find your exact match.

Debunked!

Yeesh-o-rama, have you ever been on a date with someone's statistics? It ain't pretty. I'm a big fan of the jolt you get when you see someone from across the room.

Years ago I was an editorial assistant for a microbiology journal. I was walking to lunch with some of the scientists and we passed a greenhouse. "Some plants will wilt if you go near them when you have your period," said one of the women, a visiting postdoctoral student from Spain.

"You're kidding," I said, a little disgusted.

"We forget that we're mammals." She smiled.

DATE 11 The Money Shot of Espresso

TRUE CONFESSION

If I continually have to tell men that "I'm not that kind of a girl,"
maybe it's time to look at how I present myself.

"Don't you have any friends you can set me up with?"

"Sure, a lot of the guys from work are available. They're gonna
want to have sex with you right away, though."

"On the first date?"

"Yeah, that's what porn stars do."

My friend John works as a manager for an adult film company
in the San Fernando Valley. Though I don't have much interest
in seeing close-ups of male genitalia, even if they are freakishly
proportioned, or maybe especially if they're freakishly proportioned, I am always curious about how the porn industry works.
From what I can piece together, it sounds like it is run much like
the Mafia, but without the threat of gangland-style slayings.
People are very close-knit and once you're part of the family, you
acquire what sounds suspiciously like lifetime job security. Salaries
and bonuses are far more than those of comparable jobs in other
industries, and the perks are extravagant. John had admired the
new Land Rover that was coming out for the next year and received the keys to one after his boss overheard him and then drew
his name in the office Secret Santa gift exchange.

Apparently job descriptions are fairly fluid. One day John will be organizing vendors for the Adult Entertainment Expo in Las Vegas, the next he is replacing the dining room table that collapsed during the shooting of *Guess Who Came at Dinner*, which was filmed at his home.

"Did your wife mind a porn shoot at your house?" I would ask.

"No, she did the lighting," he would answer.

As nice as it sounds to work in the porn industry—the actors seem very friendly and who doesn't like receiving nice presents that go in the driveway?—I don't think I would enjoy looking at people I don't know having sex with one another, so despite John's generous attempts to share things from work, the e-mail attachments and plain-wrapped video-size gifts he sends remain unopened.

Anyway, I had my own, so far non-pornographic career to attend to. It was New Year's Eve morning and I was walking to a coffee shop to get my last eggnog latte of the year. I slowed to glance at a bookstore window when I felt someone watching me. He was kind of good looking, with wavy, sort of feathered blond hair and bright blue eyes with crinkles around them. He was tanned and older than me, probably early forties, and wearing tight jeans and a newish black leather jacket.

"What are you doing?" the man said.

It seemed obvious to me that I was looking into the window of a bookstore, but I answered, "I'm going to have an eggnog latte," instead.

"I'll buy," he said.

I don't normally do coffee dates, as they are jittery and noncommittal, but since I just met this guy and it was technically a holiday, I made an exception.

After he brought our lattes to the little table by the window, I learned that he was retired already, and presumably wealthy. He told me that he lived in "an expensive condo." When I asked him what a young retired guy did all day, he said he e-mailed people.

While I am not opposed to men with money, there is something decidedly un–Cary Grant–like about saying that you have it point-blank. He kept trying to get a glimpse of my cleavage, but I was wearing my sweater with a big fake fur collar which shows nothing, even though everyone looks for some reason.

Since he was blunt with me about having money, I thought I would follow his lead:

"So what do you do?"

"Currently I go on dates and then write about them on a Web site and hope that strangers will send me money after they read about them."

"Yeah, porn is the only way to make money on the Internet."

I was totally put off that he not only automatically assumed my Web site was porn but that he didn't ask me what it was called, so I decided to mess with him.

Him: I'm thinking of starting up a porn site, but I need girls to model for me.

Me: That sounds so naughty I'd probably do it for free.

He knocked his eggnog latte off the table and it went flying. Splat. It glazed the tile floor, sticky, eggy, and hot. A skinny, nervous employee with glasses immediately ran over and threw a plastic yellow Caution triangle on the wet floor near us.

Me (*to the barista*): You came pretty quick. I guess you liked watching us.

Barista: Uh, no. It's part of the Starbucks Barista Safety Code to put up a cone when someone spills a drink.

Me: Ooooh, is that bare-ista with an *e*?

Barista: Tsk.

I'd seen the money shot and I was done with this scene. I politely finished my drink, packed up my ubiquitous backpack, said, "It was nice meeting you" to Spilled Latte, and left. As I was making my way home, I saw a man in a pristine gold Corvette (what else?) waving at me. He pulled over. It was him. He wanted my e-mail address. I didn't give it to him, though. I thought he was a bit of a creep. It's one thing to be a pornography professional, but this guy was strictly an amateur.

A few nights later I was at the kind of crowded party that is conducive to singed hair from errant cigarettes and instant intimacy with whomever is trapped next to you during the thirty-five-minute wait at the bar.

"I tell ya, Annie—was it Annie?—these passive Seattle men don't ask women out. It's enough to turn me into a lesbian," a red-headed woman said to me. I thought how lucky I am that I consistently have men ask for my phone number. Two hours, two cocktails, and one big struggle to get my credit card back from the bartender later, I hadn't met anyone. Was that woman right? Maybe Seattle men are passive and hard to date. Apparently I was just one comment from a potential lesbian away from losing my faith.

When I got home I opened a package that John had sent and did what I'm sure many people do after striking out at a party: I watched porn.

The only time I had ever seen adult films before, it was purely accidental. Soft-core comes on late at night on cable and sometimes I'll doze off while watching something like *Six Feet Under* and when I open my eyes I'll think: *Wow. Those two bereaved people are really comforting each other. That is one wild funeral home, but I guess it makes sense since it's supposed to be in L.A.*

Then I immediately change the channel.

I picked up the video. "You will enjoy this. It even has a story line," John had written on a Post-it.

Yeah, I'd be sure to see every moment of *Lord of the G-strings* so I wouldn't lose the thread of what I was sure would be a very complex plot.

I was surprised at how well done it was. The actors were likable and some of the lines were really witty. Even as I realized where some men get the idea to use way too much tongue and spend way too much time with breast fondling, I found myself really rooting for the usually topless heroine Dildo Saggins.

We aren't so different, she and I. Bad animation segues, a horny, drunken wizard named Smirnoff, getting caught masturbating in a forest by a voyeuristic band of men who are ripping off Monty Python . . . what woman hasn't been there?

Sure, she was looking for a magic black-lace-and-pearl G-string and I am searching for more intangible things like love and artistic satisfaction, but we are each on a personal quest, encountering lesbians along the way.

An hour later I had lost the thread of what turned out to be a very complex plot. I turned off the video.

As I got ready for bed, I felt a renewed sense of faith. I, like Dildo, would continue on my journey and would someday find my own equivalent of a magic G-string.

When I do, I will cherish it and, like her, keep it tightly clenched between my buttocks.

DATE 12 Little Twat

TRUE CONFESSION

You will never, ever hear mean things about yourself like the kind of mean things you'll hear about yourself if you post your picture and dating diary on the Internet and then get on the national news. I've been reduced to tears by eleven-year-old girls on a ballet message board.

People who read my site know that I date men I meet going about my daily life—hanging out in bars, coffee shops, or the grocery store. Those who don't read it, including several people who've interviewed me, assume that I'm looking for men to date on the Internet. Some of the people who don't read my site ask me out.

I realized that there was a pattern to the men who would write to me asking for dates. If they actually lived in my state they were generally not in Seattle but rather lived in places with names like Port Orchard.

Even if I did date men through the Web site I wouldn't date someone who lives out of town, but nonetheless strangers from places I've never heard of continued to send me letters describing their work, their hobbies, and their marital status.

More often than not they included pictures of children, their own if they were divorced, nieces and nephews or perhaps borrowed neighbor children if they were single. I suppose the intended effect was to make the men look less like serial killers, a sort of implied "See, these kids are standing next to me and they're still alive. Would you like to meet for coffee?"

When I don't respond, the second e-mail from such men is rarely suited to the children appearing in the photographs with them. In just a week's time their online personalities go through a metamorphosis worthy of Dr. Jekyll. "I enjoy cooking with friends and hiking" becomes "Your Web site is just a pathetic excuse to act like a slut." "You seem like a very interesting lady" becomes "The only thing you have going for you is your tits."

I had lunch with my friend Maureen. She is a disc jockey on a morning radio show. Like everyone I know, she had lots of questions about my love life—not my real love life necessarily, but the cartoon version of it I have posted on the Web site. Sometimes I forget and accidentally tell people how I really feel about one of my dates ("I had real hope for things working out for us and was so sad when he stopped calling and then changed his number") but it just makes everyone uncomfortable or bored. What they want are horror stories.

Since Maureen is in the public eye, fans have access to her through e-mail and by phone. She is in a more legitimate version of the position I'm in, but the feedback she gets is the same: it consists of things people would never say to her face.

"I've gotten the meanest e-mails about the TV promo of the morning team that was showing before the *Friends* reruns," she said.

I knew the one she meant. It's very . . . up. She and her colleagues always manage to sound ecstatic about the latest grocery store opening in Kent, even if they've praised the freezer section fifteen times already that day. The television spot kicks even that up a notch. It's also the only time some people have seen what they look like. Like most people who work in entertainment, Maureen is attractive and slim.

"People e-mail me and say, 'You look like shit,'" she said.

I know she's understating. People lose all sense of boundaries when they're camouflaged by an e-mail address. My real sex life is thin as a tie from the '80s, yet I've become immune to being called *whore* from the sheer repetition of hearing it.

"I tell myself it's just someone having a bad day," Maureen said.

"I tell myself that it's someone who's suffered irreversible brain damage from being run over by the short bus they were waiting for, but I guess that's the difference between us," I said.

It's the twenty-first century and yet the two best ways to cut a woman down remain calling into question her morality and her looks. And people aren't just cruel, they're specific. My hair, my skin, my belly. The only consolation is how across-the-board it is for anyone who is in the public eye at any level.

"I heard Gwen Stefani in an interview and she said she's thinking of taking the message boards off the No Doubt Web site because they're too painful to read. If they can criticize her, all platinum and lean and beautiful . . ." I said.

"Yeah, she's perfect," said Maureen.

That week I received an e-mail from a man I didn't know with the subject line "Our Date."

"We would stroll through Golden Gardens Park, stop for mimosas or fish and chips, we would dance under the stars or under the twinkle lights at the Century Ballroom, then you would tell me it's been lovely, but that you must be home early. I'd go back out dancing, this time by myself."

He sent pictures of himself wearing a felt hat and an oversized suit—endearing since the swing trend ended years ago. He included a photo of himself playing with his nephew. Something about his sweet earnestness convinced me to meet him for coffee.

He chose a funky, big bookstore and coffeehouse on a hill. I found him as soon as I walked in, a small, slight man, probably late twenties with blue eyes and a shaved head. No felt hat. I introduced myself and sat down. He was sitting behind a big, white ceramic mug of half-finished tea and reading a thick textbook about mathematics, although he said he wasn't a student, but rather a technical writer who worked as a temp. He did not offer me coffee, but instead launched into questions, his eyes alternating between darting and staring.

"Sorry, I sometimes have trouble focusing," he said. It felt like he meant something deeper than his vision.

"So, have you lived in Seattle long?" I asked.

"No, I live in Tacoma. I took the bus up."

"Isn't that kind of far?"

"It's only two hours."

"Do you want to go dancing?" he said after he finished his tea. "It's right up the hill."

It was two o'clock in the afternoon on a Tuesday and I couldn't imagine what kind of club could possibly be open, but my curiosity got to me and so we began walking. He mentioned that he used to live in New York.

"It's such a great city, why did you leave?" I said.

"Um, the economy there got bad because these two planes crashed into two buildings," he answered. "You may have heard about it?"

When I'm telling this story to friends, it's usually at this point that most people say they would have left. I did not leave, however, but instead followed him into a deserted building at the community college. We stood at the end of a hallway next to a locked room with a polished wooden floor and a mirrored wall.

"The other dancers aren't here yet," he said, pointing out the obvious. "And it's not so much dancing as free-form piling on one another to music."

I came to my senses. "I have to go. This is too weird for me."

"I warned you about the situation," he said.

"Yes, you did."

I wrote up a completely harmless, saccharine date description on my Web site, hoping to avoid the vitriol of someone whose allegiance to his medication clearly wavered.

This was my first date with someone who wrote to me on the site. Perhaps, not coincidentally, it was also my weirdest date, since no money was spent!

Today I met Mistakenly Swingin'—so called because he's a dancer with a "swing dance" look about him, but he's not that into swing. We met at a coffeehouse that Yoko Ono has been known to frequent when she's in town. Coincidentally, they were playing the *Let It Be* album. While Yoko's husband sang about digging a pony, I was starting to dig Mistakenly. He is a technical writer. He has a shaved head and pretty blue eyes. He is very funny. He did not even offer to buy me coffee. We talked about dance—he is into something called contact modern, where you apparently "just pile on one another"—I was a dancer for fifteen years and had never heard of it.

We walked to a dance place that is under a theater, but I declined to stay and dance as it was a private thing and there were no other people there yet. It was nice meeting him, though.

The men I date who know about my site usually send a nice note after they read my sugarcoated interpretation of events. I like to be especially complimentary when I know someone will be reading my report about him, so comparisons to attractive famous people and significant artists tend to get thrown around liberally.

A few days after I published the date online, I got an e-mail from Mistakenly Swingin'. I was sure he wanted to thank me for the cute write-up and what I thought was a clever Beatles reference.

"What a little twat" was all it said.

BUNK DEBUNK

Myth: If I were prettier/smarter/sluttier, this guy who's a total jerk would morph into a great guy for me.

Debunked!

Gah! It's so tempting to think this way, isn't it? Well don't.

For some reason, we women really buy into this scenario where we're responsible for how men act.

It's a crock.

If he wants you to fetch him beer while he watches football every weekend, if he is cheap with you, if he's chronically late . . . he was like that with all of his ex-girlfriends and he'll be like that with any future ones after you dump his late, cheap, beer-drinking butt.

It's not who you are, it's who he is.

DATE 13 The Mouse King

TRUE CONFESSION

He is my only good argument for meeting someone through an Internet dating diary.

I was sick of waiting for Christmas Tree to ask me out and my hints were getting broader. "I'd love to learn to snowboard," I cooed, technically not a lie because I do wish I had the guts or the motivation to learn.

"Lift tickets are pretty expensive," he said. I guess his hint about not wanting to pay for both of us was pretty broad too. "The first day's really hard. You'll be wet and crying. After that you'll either want to do it all the time or you'll never want to do it again."

"Do you think I would fall a lot?" I asked, scrambling desperately. A better question would have been: Where had my IQ run off to?

"I'd be there to catch you if you fell," he said.

One of the only ways to stay sane when you're dating a lot of different guys is to talk to your girl friends about them. One of the only ways to stay sane when you have a crazy Web site is to talk to people who have even crazier ones. I could do both with Penny, the woman I had met on the live talk show the month before.

"I just don't know about these younger men. It seems the older guys who don't appeal to me jump at the chance to make formal dates right away. The young guys drag things on for eons. Christmas Tree asks me to do things like go running with him or asks when we're going to the gym together. Would you call that asking for a date?"

"Well, your Web site isn't called Running With Amy, so no, I wouldn't call it a date."

"Even if he has dark, dark blue eyes?"

Penny and I had another talk show invitation and this time it was national. Montel Williams's producer had e-mailed both of us, so we got together to discuss it.

I was unsure about going on *Montel Williams*. I had never seen the show and feared it involved brawling and chair throwing and a long legal release exempting Montel from all of it. The producer also wanted me to bring one of my dates with me. My actor friends immediately declined and started screening their calls. I didn't want to take any of my former dates or ruin my chances with any current prospects by involving them in the circus that my love life was becoming, so I was stuck.

I could think of one guy to bring. He had written to me at the site, so he obviously already knew about it. He was a jewelry photographer who seemed fairly normal when I talked to him on the phone. The only problem was that we already had an on-again, off-again relationship and we hadn't met yet. He had called to ask me out and then wouldn't set a date. He confessed later that he got intimidated because I sounded "overly professional and newscaster-ish" on the phone.

When he called again he told me he realized he was just being silly and remembered that I was just some weird, crazy Internet chick and asked me out again. I went Scarlett O'Hara and told him "I never give a man a second chance to disappoint me."

I reconsidered and called him, amending my declaration with ". . . unless I'm asked to be on a talk show. If you come there's an all-expenses-paid weekend in New York in it for you."

The magic of television got me my first date with a man my

readers and I would later come to know as the Mouse King. Montel would not share a similar fate, however, as he ended up canceling on all of us and then I heard rumors that he was getting canceled himself, which I'm not sure was a coincidence.

We met at a bistro near my house with a fireplace and a wooden floor (the Mouse King and I, not Montel Williams and I). "I love this place because it's not just all adults. There are families with kids. You don't see that as much at places that have a bar like this," he said. He was big and tall and bearlike with smart, square black glasses and curly dishwater hair.

"I brought you something." He handed me a thin package wrapped in brown paper with a bow made of straw and red ribbon. It was a book on writing he thought I'd like called *Bird by Bird*. I was touched. Hopefully things wouldn't degenerate into profane e-mails with this one. Although, actually, perhaps they would be going from me to him.

"One of my complaints about your Web site is when you write about movies. It has nothing to do with dating, and I hadn't seen any of the ones you mentioned recently and you spoiled the endings." In my own defense, the mother ending up with the Hugh Grant character in *About a Boy* was never really even implied, so to a thinking person it wasn't exactly a big spoiler.

"Another thing is that you need new pictures and not the scary one you have up with the pink bar over your eyes."

I had originally done that for the sake of privacy, a bit of a moot point since the press had dug up my last name in December. Okay, it wasn't so much "dug up" as they asked me and I told them.

"You have to let me take pictures of you. If I can make jewelry look good, imagine what I could do with you."

He had redeemed himself and did so again by ordering a bottle of pinot noir from California. I had crab cakes and he had a Caesar salad in deference to my small meal, although he said he wanted the steak. Since I didn't know for sure if it was a dinner date, I had had a slice of pizza beforehand.

I told him I'm going to call him Mouse King because he played that part in *The Nutcracker* recently, although he's not a dancer.

He's perpetually working on a historical novel that remains perpetually unfinished. "I never thought of writing a book," I said. "I guess in a way I'm writing one now with the Web site, though."

He had just gotten back from Louisiana.

"When I went to New Orleans I didn't even tell my friends who live there I was in town. I brought my bass and sat in with these old jazz guys in a little club," he said.

"I always wanted to be a musician, too," I said. "When I lived in L.A. I was trying to sing and play guitar and write songs. Then I realized I suck."

"So you just gave up?"

"Well, I recorded a CD and then I gave up."

"You have the Web site and your own CD?" he said. "You take things further than I do."

Our conversation naturally turned to one of my favorite topics, Europe.

"When I was in Italy, rather than do the typical tourist cities, I threw down a map and tossed a coin and told myself I'd go wherever it landed. I ended up in a small town south of Sardinia," he said.

"I love that," I said, because I do.

"You take things further than I do, though," he repeated. "You live your whole life that way."

DATE 14 The $6 Bottle of Wine

TRUE CONFESSION

When I told one of my girl friends what happened on this date, she immediately brought up a charming scene from a movie where a guy asks Marisa Tomei if she wants to listen to some music and then shows up at her house with a record player. My friend suggested that I rent the video to get perspective on my situation. In the movie the guy ends up being from another planet. This is why I don't take advice from my friends.

This date answers the long-standing question: When is the right time to tell a guy you like, "Hey, I am going on fifty dates and writing about them on the Internet"? That answer being: when the people from TV force you to.

I finally had my first official date with my big crush, Christmas Tree. It was textbook playing-hard-to-get-but-not-so-hard-that-you-don't-get-gotten. I had purposely been avoiding him as a ploy to make him miss me. I knew he must like me or he wouldn't have helped me get my Christmas tree and I realized that it was my casual availability at the grocery store where he worked that was causing him to take me for granted and not ask me out. I bought my food elsewhere for two weeks, then breezed in one Sunday afternoon. I waved hello, but did not seek him out even then. I purposely went to a different line. He came and took my basket from me while the checker who was starting to check me out looked like "What the fuck?"

"I never get to see her," he said to her.

"You should give me your number so we can go out sometime," he immediately said, ripping a piece of paper off the receipt roll.

It was so easy, third-grade math to a college freshman.

When he called just a few days later to invite me out for a drink I was thrilled. The only problem was that a local NBC news show was doing a story on me and wanted to come with us, and Christmas Tree didn't know about the site. I knew the day would come when I'd be smoked out because of the media, but I was still totally unprepared.

I didn't know if I should (a) just 'fess up and tell the truth, (b) cancel the date, (c) cancel the interview, or (d) pretend not to notice the camera crew and when he mentioned them say, "Oh, I thought they were with you."

I left him the message: "I need to talk to you about Sunday and you're probably going to want to cancel on me, so call me back."

A full day later, he did call back and I gave a charcoal sketch of the situation—I said I have a sort of *Sex and the City*–type column on the Internet and that NBC is doing a story on it and can they send a camera crew to film us having a drink?

"That doesn't sound like something I'd like at all," he said. He didn't ask why NBC would be following an unemployed writer around, but as I said, his simplicity was part of the attraction. "So where are we going on Sunday night?" I said. "I know a great wine bar in Ballard." It was such a cute place, a sunken living room with couches and great wines by the glass, so warm and cozy. I was excited.

"Let's decide that on Sunday," he said.

I called NBC and broke the news that they would be dateless. They asked if I'd call him back to see if they could just film the back of his head. I promised them I would call him to ask and then of course didn't.

I didn't care about NBC, though. I was finally getting what I wanted: a real date with Christmas Tree.

He buzzed me from outside and was right on time, which I love.

I told him I'd be right down. He said, "Um, no, that's okay, I'll come up."

He had a bottle of wine with him.

"Is that for me?" I asked. I was reaching for my coat.

"I asked if you wanted to have a glass of wine, so here I am and I brought wine," he said.

What?

"I thought we were going out," I said.

"I'm not really dressed for it," he said. He was in nice black pants and a button-down shirt—he could have attended the opera in what he was wearing. "I guess there was a miscommunication."

Miscommunication. When he said on Wednesday that he wasn't sure where we were going, and that we could decide on Sunday, I guess he was deciding between my living room and my bedroom.

There's a point in every relationship where the decision is made as to which way things will go, a tipping point, a power struggle, a miniature battle of the sexes played out by two. It was not just about staying in or going out but about the way things would be if we got involved. Men everywhere rose to their feet and did the wave as I conceded defeat and took the bottle of wine out of its sad paper bag. It was $6 wine at best, I didn't even want to think about what it cost after his employee discount. I grudgingly poured two glasses. I've heard that when you toast, you have to look into each other's eyes or your sex life will be bad. We did not toast.

I've always thought of Christmas Tree as uncomplicated, but discovered that he actually has lots of different interests: investing, his boat, his dirt bike, snowboarding trips with his budzos, buying houses, $100-a-throw roulette—but he assured me he doesn't like to waste his money on anything stupid. I felt myself being shoved into the "anything stupid" category.

I was nice, but quiet and distracted the whole evening. Being passive-aggressive is always the right choice. I had two CDs already in, but didn't bother to put on any more once they had played. I didn't turn on the TV or suggest that we watch any of my videos. We sat on the couch and faced forward like people sitting next to each other on a plane.

"I sometimes talk to Kitty who works for you," I said, by way of non-conversation.

"She's a talker," he said.

"There's always one person that everyone at work kind of shuts the office door and laughs about," I said.

"Yeah, that would be Kitty," he said.

I had time to notice that he's not just pleasant looking, he's really handsome. He's a frat boy, though. It's not so much that he was dorky enough to show up at my house with a $6 bottle of chardonnay in a brown paper bag; it's that when I was obviously uncomfortable with just sitting in my apartment all night, he insisted we stay anyway.

When he finally left and I closed the door, relieved, I found a bright spot to the evening: NBC wasn't here to see it.

Political demonstrations were everywhere and I was afraid of getting caught on a magazine news show not knowing enough about current affairs. I frantically read up on the history of the Middle East and tried to come up with an intelligent response about Israelis and Palestinians in case they asked me any questions about how I thought things should be handled there. It's a complex issue, but I was a political science major, after all.

The next day, the people from NBC interviewed me at my apartment. They sent a cameraman and a reporter. The cameraman moved my kitchen chairs into the living room so the reporter and I were facing each other. It was like a low-budget Barbara Walters special. She had questions for me written on recipe cards.

"Aren't you *embarrassed*? No, let me try that again. Aren't *you* embarrassed? Can you get the back of her head in that shot and I'll ask 'Aren't you embarrassed?' again."

So much for brushing up on the history of Palestine.

"Now how in the world did you think up calling men by made-up names? Why did you do that? Wait, why did you *do* that?"

The cameraman and the reporter obviously could not stand each other. At one point he banged her head really hard with his camera and I'm pretty sure it was on purpose. She made an overly big deal about how much it hurt and implied that he was clumsy, stupid, and bad at his job with her body language. It was terrible and awkward.

They then took me to a coffee shop so they could show me "interacting with people and getting dates." They filmed me walking in and ordering a latte. Of course, true to character, I didn't have enough money, so I whispered to the guy behind the counter, "Dude, I don't have enough money. I'll pay ya later." He said not to worry about it and handed me back my $2 as if he were giving me change.

Meanwhile, the reporter was telling any man who would listen about my site. She whispered to me that she had found a man who was willing to meet me. She motioned to a guy with a gray beard who I'm quite sure was homeless. People were fleeing to get away from the camera. I sat by myself at a tiny table in the now-empty room, feeling like Gulliver and trying to look like it was natural to have a camera glued to me.

After the interview I went back to pay for my coffee as I had promised. The guy who made my latte said he had heard of Dating Amy before. I told the woman he was working with that I was going on fifty dates.

"Wow. Are you totally disillusioned yet?" she said.

The next day I wrote a cute, funny entry on my Web site about the segment I filmed. I put up a picture of the reporter posed next to the camera with the caption "There's a Media Frenzy in My Living Room!" I talked about people running from the camera at the coffee shop and gave an honest answer about what really embarrasses me: doing television interviews.

I was excited to get an e-mail from the reporter that day. Maybe she wanted to do a follow-up interview.

"Media frenzy, huh?" her e-mail said. "If you're embarrassed by interviews, then you shouldn't do them anymore."

She then sent me a second e-mail that said: "And take my picture down, too."

I was crushed. I wrote an apology to everyone at NBC who had had the misfortune to have to deal with me.

"Pfft, don't worry about it," said my friend Maureen who works on a morning radio show. "There's always one person at work that everyone kind of laughs about after they shut their office door."

When I got home there was an e-mail from the producer at NBC. He said that everyone at the station thought the write-up was really funny. "But then, *we* got it."

BUNK DEBUNK

Myth: It's a man's world (and they start 'em young). (Part I)

Bunked!

I was coming back from the thrift store on the bus the other morning and it was crowded, so I sat in back. The back of the bus is much more social than the grim, forward-facing seats in front. I think it's because it's set up like a conversation area in a living room. It's like being at a party, but without drinks, appetizers, or people you'd ever want to see again. There was a couple with a boy and girl, each about seven years old, and a guy who I think was their teacher, all sitting across from me. The kids were named Darius and Toby but I couldn't tell which was which.

"You need to start a Girls' Club if he won't let you in the Boys' Club," said the mom to Darius or Toby.

"Eh, the Boys' Club always seems to unravel right away, anyway," said the dad.

"Yeah, after they do 'pull my finger' there isn't much else to say and it falls apart," said the teacher guy.

"No, one of them gets a girlfriend and it falls apart," said the dad, laughing.

Like most women who've attended grade school, high school, college, or any work environment, I'm more than familiar with the Boys' Club. But as a female, I'm not quite clear on the rules. It seems that in the workplace, it's Have a Penis, Make 23 Percent More. When guys have a brutal falling-out at work, they still manage to grab a beer or a game of B-ball with each other that night and everything's okay. Does swooping in on someone else's girlfriend work the same way?

I have a ton of male friends. The fact that I can't even get a consistent answer to this question indicates to me just how impermeable the Boys' Club really is.

No wonder men rule the world.

DATE 15 My Two Biggest Assets as a Writer

TRUE CONFESSION

This date felt very much like I was attending it simply because I had RSVP'd. I found out a year later that the guy felt the exact same way. Hmph.

"You should put pictures of yourself giving blow jobs on the site instead of that crappy picture you have up."

"You'd get more donations with no picture at all."

It was six in the morning my time. While I had my first cup of coffee, Drew and Mike of WRIF in Detroit had the distinct advantage of a time zone difference. They had been up for hours and were wired. They peppered me with questions about masturbation ("No comment"), my cup size ("36C"), what I'm like in bed ("um, athletic?"). They asked me if I drink, if I do drugs, and if I'm horny. They asked me if I'd go topless on the site, if I'd give hand jobs on the site, and if I'd at least start *describing* sex on the site ("No to most of those").

They told me that I'll get nowhere with good writing, but that some nice titty action will take me far.

More disturbing than their suggestion that I become a foot-fetish model was the fact that even these Howard Stern types were asking questions of what I wanted in a man that I hadn't asked of myself. What was wrong with me? Surely "What are you looking for?" and "What sort of man do you like?" shouldn't have me short-circuiting a synapse like it was the last round of *Jeopardy!* but instead should have been something I've instinctively known since I was twelve like a normal woman.

"So you've been an outspoken critic about U.S. international policies. Are you saying it's okay for people from other countries to ram planes into our buildings? How would you deal with the situation in the Middle East?"

Aha! Finally.

Later that day, I had a different sort of interview. I went out on a blind date with a man who wrote to me on Match.com and works for a local television station. We met at a Thai restaurant near my house and he was waiting for me when I got there. I had the appetite of a lion, but tried to demurely select a piece of egg roll that was already at the table. They brought our hot-and-sour soup and I scarfed that down, too.

I had the chicken cashew combination (which included pad Thai and rice) and he had the red curry. We both ordered level two of spicy—yeah, right. Mine was so hot that my eyes were watering, my nose was running, and I was choking. My voice sounded like Peter Brady's as I answered the same sort of questions from my date that the guys on the morning radio show had asked. Except obviously the ones about my bra size and favorite sexual positions and whether or not I like the pubic hair of red-headed men, etc. He did mention dicks but I quickly realized he meant Dick's, the burger place around the corner which is where he said he had his first job.

At the end of the date he did not say, "I'll call you," but I've found that may or may not mean he'll call . . .

Which of course he didn't . . . for over a year anyway.

BUNK DEBUNK

Myth: Deep down, in their heart of hearts, all men are, for lack of a better word, pervs.

Bunked!

I was working as a spokesmodel at a big food convention one weekend. One of the reasons that handing out food samples is called spokesmodeling is so that the people who are doing it can feel good about being paid $12 an hour to assault total strangers with product information they don't want.

Lacking any real models to look at, the men I was working with turned their attention to giving comments and a numerical rating to every woman who walked past our booth. Men are far more generous in their appraisal of women's looks than women are. Ladies, feel free to tack on two points to whatever you think you are on a scale of one to ten. Men don't often yell out numbers like my co-models, but I sense that the sentiment is always there.

The next morning there was this odd little guy sitting next to me at Starbucks. The kind of guy you'd expect to expose himself. He ran outside without his coat, although there was snow on the ground, and had a stupid grin on his face as he looked down the street. While he was outside, one of the baristas came over to me and asked if the little man was creeping me out. Since it was *I* who had sat next to *him*, I felt it would be rude to say one way or another, so I just shrugged. She said that the reason he ran outside was to stare at some woman who had just walked out. When he came back in, she asked him to leave because he was making people uncomfortable.

Apparently you can get kicked out of Starbucks for

ogling. They have a very strict no-creepiness policy, unless it's the corporate, pro-gentrification kind of creepiness, in which case you can head up their western sales division.

I was thinking about both these incidents and I suspect that it's not just that my fellow food samplers were immature (although they were) or that the guy at Starbucks was creepy (although he was). It's that men are preoccupied with women. It's another Dating Amy exclusive: MEN DRIVEN BY SEX, SOME HIDE IT BETTER THAN OTHERS.

The difference between married bankers in Armani suits who don't look at women and drunk guys on the street who blatantly gawk at them is only one of social boundaries. The crazier guys just openly express what every man is thinking. One has a $1 million home, one has a heated sidewalk grate, but their feelings toward miniskirts are identical.

It's endearing in a way. Inside every man is a little pervert just begging to be booted out of Starbucks.

DATE 16 Fire Walk with Me Where There Are No Porta Pottis

TRUE CONFESSION

I might have known that anyone who would scare me by calling it hiking instead of walking would not fit in with my dreamy fantasy world.

I've always had the ability to completely and utterly suspend disbelief. While others point out flaws in a movie's logic or technical execution, to me a long-lost husband, presumed dead for years, who arrives by a small aircraft that he manages to fly with no previous lessons just in time to save his family from the serial killer sounds about right.

I was beside myself when Unrefrigerated Sandwich Recommender from the health food store invited me to go hiking in Twin Peaks. Of course the area is not really called that, but my imagination had already run away. And I had even been there before.

The lodge had a cavernous, deserted lobby. Its locked rooms held secrets and stories never to be told except in a whisper or in a dream. Mist rose as if in slow motion from the pounding waterfall beneath the lodge. Beautiful waitresses with ruby lips and haunted expressions served an endless stream of coffee and slices of cherry pie to pale men in suits at a diner. A woman-child sang songs that rose above the green velvet pine forests which were filled with death and mystery and hope. The town itself danced to a slow, narcotic waltz in a melancholy minor key.

In reality the town is called North Bend. It is located about twenty minutes outside of Seattle. The diner burned down due to arson in 2000 and was rebuilt. There, average-looking waitresses wear T-shirts that have pictures of cherry pie slices on them. The walls are papered with TV stills from the site's heyday. The lodge, actually a five-star hotel, has a lobby that is neither bleak nor quiet, but is instead filled with noisy tourists and their loud floral prints. The waterfall provides a jolt of recognition and is quite frequently blocked by the heads of a hundred tourists, which should be expected, but is always a surprise to me the first time I see any well-known attraction. "Gee, all these people had the exact same idea as we did, and on a beautiful Sunday afternoon, no less."

The first time I went to the town, I went with a girl friend. It was Indian summer and the trees looked like they were strung with red and yellow crepe paper. We took a table near the window and ordered Sunday brunch. My coffee came with a side of unsweetened whipped cream and chocolates and nut bits. I asked for catsup for my hash browns and they gave me my own little bottle, like the tiny liquor bottles on planes. My girl friend ordered a Bloody Mary, so I had orange juice and champagne. I had a $17 garden omelet. Sometimes when you get a $17 omelet you're paying for the location, but in this case the omelet was actually worth $1 per bite.

The rush of the water against the October gold-leaf-and-pine hillside was lovely.

On the way home she surprised me by taking me to a winery— Chateau St. Michelle. It was a day courtesy of Hollywood.

While my acceptance of fantasy is great for movies and television, it wreaks havoc on my love life.

Unrefrigerated Sandwich claimed to be unable to use MapQuest, so he asked me to meet him at a pretty market near my house. He looked great, but let me buy my own $1.25 coffee at the grocer's, which seemed ridiculous to me since he even waited in line with me.

The plan was to go hiking and then have lunch. We drove past hills of pine trees, cows grazing, and mountains capped with bits of snow.

"Where are the bathrooms?" I asked after we hiked a bit. He looked at me like I had brought a dozen Louis Vuitton bags on an overnight camping trip, when of course in reality I would only bring four or five, tops. "There are no bathrooms," he said, "can't you wait?" "Uh, no." We had to go back to the car and drive to a nearby town so I could use the restroom at a gas station.

We got in the vicinity of the lodge, but parked far away, along the street because he didn't want to pay for parking at the hotel.

We walked all the way down to the bottom of the falls and I could feel the mist on my face.

The walk back up the hill was steep and we were hungry by that time. The obvious place to eat was the lodge and as we passed it on the long walk back to the car, Unrefrigerated Sandwich commented, "You can't eat there, it's so expensive."

I reminisced about the tiny catsup bottle. That feeling of being cut off from a good meal bothered me. Was this indicative of his worldview? I had been there with a girl friend and everyone knows that two women have less disposable income than a man and a woman because of the pay gap. The only couple combination better equipped to dine at a really nice place is a gay male couple. It's simple economics.

Unrefrigerated Sandwich knew of a cute place for lunch near the cherry pie diner, though. The bar was made from cut logs and there was a fire burning. I had a chicken breast sandwich with some exotic sour cream sauce and steak fries. I'm a whore for catsup and will basically put it on anything, so I am thrilled at any opportunity to have fries. He had a veggie burger and a nice salad.

He complained about work (which was tolerable), talked about the cool sabbaticals he's had from work (which was thrilling), and fretted about the possibility of the economy getting worse, even though he had a job and I hadn't worked since I moved to Seattle. I wondered where his sense of pride in being competent and masculine had disappeared to. It was a bigger mystery than Laura Palmer's death and you could be sure I'd be writing about it in my own diary, which, unlike hers, was not at all secret.

He did treat for lunch, but I couldn't help but notice the contrast between my two experiences at the falls. Why was my female friend more successful in traditionally masculine endeavors than my date was? One could use a map, pick me up at my house, take me out to one of the best meals I've ever had, and surprise me with a wine-tasting expedition. The other couldn't navigate the five additional blocks to my apartment, positioned us as orphans with our noses pressed up against the glass of the beautiful restaurant, and vented and processed about money and finances all through lunch. The role reversal was as backward as a dancing dwarf.

Afterward he asked to come in and use my bathroom and what could I say? It was such an obvious ploy to get into my apartment. When he was done we had an awkward tango in the entryway. I practically pushed him out and breathed a sigh of relief with my back against the door after I shut it abruptly behind him.

I didn't know what I was doing anymore with men. I had become the kind of woman who doesn't kiss on the third date.

"We know, we know. You don't even kiss on the third date and we're more masculine and competent than the men you go out with. You're making us all sick," my girl friends said.

DATE 17 Can Men and Women Just Be Friends? Probably Not If They're Straight.

TRUE CONFESSION

After those respectable dates and meals and gifts from other men, what it really took to get my sexual resolve to crumble like an almond cookie at a greasy Chinese place was Christmas Tree offering to come over and fix my stereo (which still makes that funny buzzing noise, by the way).

I still couldn't believe that on our first date Christmas Tree had shown up with a paper bag of wine.

I began to tell myself the lies that every woman must tell herself when she's physically attracted to someone with whom things aren't going as planned.

Maybe, as a magazine article I read recently suggested, he was the kind of guy who woos a woman by doing things for her, rather than through dinner and drinks or jewelry giving. "I'm sure that's it," said my friend Sabrina, who coincidentally was the one who told me to rent the Marisa Tomei movie about the alien with the record player when this same guy brought over a bottle of wine rather than taking me out.

I decided to give him a second chance.

I don't know what I was thinking. I know there was something about him fixing my stereo; it was buzzing—still does, actually.

I had some chardonnay open and so we finished the bottle. "I should go get more wine," he said. "I have a bottle in my truck, but it's white zinfandel."

Why would someone carry wine in their truck? More important, why does white zinfandel exist?

"You're going to look at my stereo?"

"That's right, the reason I'm here."

He had just gotten back from a trip to New Orleans, the land of hurricanes and "show your tits." I offered wine and the opportunity to see other women's tits—we watched one of my *Sex and the City* videos.

The episodes covered circumcision, men looking at other women, sex with movie stars, and dating straight men who seem gay. You know, typical date conversation.

"What is she wearing? That's awful!" he said, referring to Sarah Jessica Parker's Oscar the Grouch pajamas which she was wearing as casual wear. It was the longest sentence uttered for the rest of the night.

He hit me with a pillow from my couch. Lightly. And again.

"Cut it out," I said.

He pulled me to him and kissed the sliver of bare belly between my pants and black tank top. I still wasn't 100 percent positive he was attracted to me. He slid up and grazed my cleavage with his tongue. I was wearing a black lace push-up bra and when I looked down, there were three flesh-colored rounds: my breasts and the top of his shaved head. He still hadn't looked at me. I closed my eyes and he moved up even a little more. I could feel him breathing. Our lips were so close, almost touching, yet we still hadn't kissed. Luscious torture. When we finally did kiss, it was hard and fast.

"Put your arms around me," he said. My legs were already around him. He put his hands on my butt and stood in one easy motion. I still had my eyes closed. I was being carried but there was no effort on his part. All that time at the gym.

I love that time before you have sex when it feels inevitable—
"a force greater than us took over" and all that. It's as if life is happening in slow motion and all decisions are out of your hands.

Our clothes were off in a couple of moments. God, his body
was so muscular. Like a Greek statue. There was nothing to grab
on to, no hair on his head or body and no fat. He put two fingers
inside me. His hands were big. It felt incredible. "You're so wet.
Do you want me inside you?" I couldn't answer in words. "Do you
want me inside you?"

I always have a beat of hesitation when I'm first naked and
vulnerable.

"Have you been tested for AIDS?" I stalled.

"Yeah, I'm fine. Where's the rubber?"

I dug into my nightstand drawer, empty except for a box of
almost-expired condoms and two dating self-help books with titles
too embarrassing to display on my bookshelf. I tore off a condom
and tossed it at him. He looked very big to me, but then I hadn't
been with anyone since I moved to Seattle.

I felt a shock of good pain. He was the size of a beer can. It was
more like he was thrusting at me than in me. It felt good and it
hurt, but we weren't fitting—all the time I spend at the gym.

I was adapting to his body already, though, I thought. Determined. I knew I could make this work. I reached down to somehow help him in with my hand and realized he wasn't even
one-third of the way in.

"Maybe if I got on top," I said. He seemed pretty doubtful, but I
thought the weight of my body might . . . Nope, I was a foot in
the air like a circus performer. This was just getting silly.

We tried a little more but after my moans turned plaintive, he
stopped. I immediately curled up like a bug. He sat next to me and
laid his hand on my hip. My body felt shocked.

"Is that it?" I said, exhausted.

"Yep," he said. "I thought you wanted me to stop."

"I did."

"That's what I thought."

"You don't at least want to jerk off?" I said. Ever the hostess.

He laughed. "Nope."

"Does this happen to you often?" I said.

He didn't answer. He was dressed already and leaning against my bedroom wall.

"I'm really freaked out. Has this happened to you before? I know it's me," I said.

"Yeah, it happens sometimes. It'll be better next time I come over. Or the time after that."

He had to put women on installment plans, literally. At least we had tentative plans for another date.

"I almost forgot, I brought these back from New Orleans for you."

It was a string of Mardi Gras beads; they were like tiny green Christmas ornaments. He set them down quietly on my nightstand. Our relationship had already changed; he would normally just toss them at me.

I guess I was wrong, he is a jewelry-expressive guy.

Due to extreme procrastination, I had let my driver's license expire in December, which meant I had to take a road test for the first time since I was sixteen. I passed with 80 percent, but the elderly gentleman who tested me said he docked points because I didn't once check my blind spot.

That also seemed to be a problem in my personal life. Christmas Tree brought up issues (and one other thing) that I hadn't had to deal with on the site yet. I had painted myself into a corner with snow-white paint. I couldn't very well have a lover and continue going on the fifty dates—I mean, I could, but it seemed unfair to the guys who were buying me dinner, getting written about on the Internet, and not getting any action. I didn't want to get into an exclusive relationship, either, unless I wanted most of the date write-ups to be about eating Thai takeout and watching videos. I didn't want to write about my sex life as it would have meant I'd have to change the name of the site to Something-else-ing Amy.

Did I have to be celibate to maintain my respectability? Was respectability even an option for someone who writes about their love life and begs for cash on the Internet?

When I started Dating Amy, friends, and then later talk show hosts, asked me, "What if you meet someone and fall in love?" I didn't have an answer for them.

My blind spot is I never really thought I would need one.

Christmas had been calling a lot since our tryst and I'd been dodging his calls since I didn't know what I wanted. As I was getting the answer to the question "How many apartment managers does it take to change a lightbulb?" (two, apparently), he called again. My one apartment manager was getting me all riled up about my writing by telling me that his son is a published author. I had a renewed enthusiasm about my Web site. I suddenly didn't feel ready to be with one person, I was probably going to be a big published writer. Christmas was obviously crazy about me and it felt cruel to keep ignoring him. While my apartment managers were thirty-five minutes into Project Lightbulb, I decided to put the boy out of his anguish and answer the phone.

"Are you avoiding me?"

"A little . . ."

"Thought so. I want to see you."

"I'm not sure . . . the thing is, I see other people and I can't get involved with you and see other people at the same time."

"Why not? I do," he said.

He told me he wanted to see others. He wanted to see others naked. That is so much worse than the kind of casual dating I do! There's no way I could get involved with him knowing that he was sleeping with other women.

"Why would it have to be exclusive?" he said. "Haven't you ever had a friend you've had sex with? That could be us."

God.

"I can't be with just one person," he said.

"Ever? Why not?" At this point it didn't really matter since he didn't want to be committed to me, but I couldn't look away from the twisted wreckage.

"I don't know. I don't even want to think about why," he said.

He was on his cell phone, driving.

"I'm taking you through a tunnel, Amy."

He had said that night he had a bottle of white zinfandel in his truck. What kind of tacky women was he banging? At least I got chardonnay. This couldn't be happening. Eight sisters, no wonder he was so good at reading women. I hadn't stood a chance.

That night I slept for four hours. I couldn't stop crying. I was shocked at how bad I felt. And then how alive. It was like my heart was this pomegranate someone broke open and all these gorgeous red seeds tumbled out.

I felt like the guy from *American Beauty*. Not the middle-aged man who was lusting after the cheerleader, but the video maker who said, "Sometimes there's so much beauty in the world I feel like I can't take it." I did not see any plastic bags dancing in the wind, but the cherry petals in the parking lot of the Korean grocer whirled around like little pink cyclones.

The spring weather refused to reflect my mood, but was instead ridiculously beautiful. Because of all the rain, the trees and flowers looked like green and red and purple neon lights when the sun shone, as it had been doing relentlessly.

As easy as it had been to accidentally on purpose run into Christmas Tree before, it was now just as hard to hide from him. There were areas of the neighborhood that were clearly unsafe and to be avoided at all costs. That morning I had had to go to three stores before I could find one that would sell me a roll of quarters, since showing up at his store was far too risky.

I couldn't believe that a week before I was dodging his calls because I didn't know how to tell him I still wanted to see other guys. What a difference an enthusiastic "Great, I still want to see other people too" makes.

Just when I most wanted to crawl under a quiet rock somewhere, network TV was rerunning past interviews I had taped for the Web site. When you first do an interview, it's like the beginning of a romance. There is a courtship. They thank you profusely. They tell you exactly when the show will be aired. They send you a nice tape of the interview. After that it's every man for himself and they can run it at any time with no warning whatsoever. I had had two interviews shown in as many weeks. People were cheerily e-mailing me saying they caught me on television the other night:

From: Katrina
Date: October 3, 2003
Subject: read me!!

Hi . . . i was just watching the news and I am quite intrigue with this site. sorry but guys who are smart enough would not even spend a minute with you . . . and besides you don't look like Barbie who has everything . . .

Isn't there some sort of halfway house for brokenhearted Internet writers where they can plan their next move in a clean, safe environment? Preferably someplace they won't be filmed, unfavorably compared to plastic dolls, or run into any ex-lovers.

DATE 18 Tiptoe Through the Tulips

TRUE CONFESSION

There's something both thrilling and comforting about a man who shows up on a Sunday morning with two cups of coffee and a full tank of gas.

After the Christmas Tree debacle, I needed to get at least a little way out of town, so when the Mouse King asked me if I'd like to get together "but not for a date you'll write about" (yeah, right), I suggested seeing the tulip fields partway between Seattle and Canada. They only bloom in April.

We had agreed that he would pick me up really early, at 8:00 a.m., and he called at around 7:30 to see if I wanted coffee and to make sure I wasn't passed out somewhere. I wasn't, and asked for a tall drip with lots of milk.

Many green fields and weathered farmhouses and an hour of great conversation later, we reached some cute prefab gardens with fake little windmills and flowers in perfect order like flowers would never be. Some of the hybrids were so hybrid they didn't look like tulips anymore.

We drove to where the fields were and began walking toward them through the mud. The colors are like a box of crayons, and if you wander into them far enough, you're wading in a knee-deep sea of red and purple and yellow.

"I don't know what I'm doing with my project," I said. "I don't know what my own point is. People write to me and ask for pictures of my boobs. It doesn't feel very literary."

"Well, you must have learned something about dating, about relationships."

"Nope. I think it may be that the most meaningful relationship I'm having is the one between me and my readers."

"That's it! 'I'm going on fifty dates and I'm taking you with me,' just like it says on your site."

It was nice being with him, being able to talk about my writing to someone. I had said on my Web site that my first date with him was one of the best first dates I've had. He wrote me that it was one of the nicer ones he had ever had too, but he couldn't date a woman who was determined to go on thirty-seven more dates. He was willing to see me, but was boycotting official dates of any kind with me.

I rhapsodized about the incredible colors of the tulips against the smoky blue mountains and distant red farmhouses. "Isn't it amazing?"

"Yeah, sure . . . actually I'm color-blind."

"And you took me all this way to see flowers?"

Our shoes and pants muddy, we stopped at a diner in a small town for breakfast. I had a Denver omelet and Mouse had a Greek one.

"I hate tomato juice," he said as he finished a big glass of it.

"Then why'd you order it?"

"I like the feeling I get after drinking it."

Then he said, "I grew up in a place like this."

"You're kidding. You're from a rural area?"

"I'm from a farm. My parents still live there."

"Mending fences, raising livestock, growing crops. Not sure I've dated a farm boy. It's very wholesome. I think it makes me more wholesome by proxy."

"People will still write to you and ask to see your tits," he said.

DATE 19 Unrefrigerated Sandwich: The Return

TRUE CONFESSION

If a guy dithers around about which restaurant to go to and tells me to pick, I'll probably choose someplace more expensive than what he was thinking.

My head is on a strange pillow and I am lying on my back with my eyes closed. My legs are splayed. I am wearing black fishnet stockings and patent leather Italian heels. There is a candle flickering next to me and I feel warm wax being dripped on my skin.

I had never had my eyebrows done before, but it's fabulous. I now have aristocratic arches I've never been able to achieve with tweezers, a shaky hand, and a picture of Heather Locklear taped to my bathroom mirror.

The purpose of the beautification was to cheer me up. I was still a little down about Christmas Tree, but there's nothing to perk a girl up like having hair ripped out of her skin by its roots, so I got the wax.

I promised myself I would linger in public for at least fifteen minutes before I went home to sulk, and in that brief span I ran into Unrefrigerated Sandwich, the guy from the health food store who had taken me to Twin Peaks.

Like rain in winter and Christmas decorations in August, men from my past always come around again. He wasted no time booking me for a Friday night dinner.

He is a cross between a swashbuckling West Coast bachelor and a fretting old woman asking if there is an extra charge for soda crackers with her matzo ball soup at a New York deli.

We decided upon a tiny, romantic restaurant upstairs from the Sanitary Market Building in Pike Market. We passed a match-maker's office where a golden retriever was asleep next to his food dish and blocking the entryway. The owner had once approached my singles-party-throwing friend Anastasia about buying her busi-ness, but the sleeping dog told me that Anastasia had made yet another good decision by declining.

The restaurant is famous for having great food and four tables, so we sat at the counter where we were served by a man named Paul who had a ponytail. I had a glass of chardonnay and pan-seared halibut with finger potatoes and different, exotic olives I'd never had, ever. He had catfish with gourmet barbecue sauce and gourmet coleslaw. The fish was like butter.

He told me online dating stories about how women told him he was the best-looking man they had met online. How women would invite him over to their houses to meet. He said one woman had him come over because she couldn't go out because of a broken leg.

"I thought it was weird," he said. "You'd think that she could take a break from dating to recuperate."

I thought it was weirder to invite a stranger from the Internet into your home if you're a woman living alone, especially if you're incapacitated.

"Isn't that sort of unsafe?" I said.

"Nah, I'm six foot five and I'm big," he said.

"No, I meant for her."

"She could tell I was a nice guy." He was indignant.

It was one of the best meals I've had in Seattle. It was astonish-ing, spectacular, the cocaine of meals . . . with the inevitable crash.

"Do you have a couple singles?" he asked.

My mind slowly registered that he was referring to money and not the marital status of any other men I had lined up.

We owed another $1.67 on the bill. But then a horrible thought occurred to me . . . he wanted me to leave the tip, too.

I numbly threw in the $6, which was my lunch money for the next day, but that only left a 10 percent tip.

"I only have hundred-dollar bills," he explained.

"Why don't you break one?" I explained.

"I'm going on a fly-fishing trip in the morning (see, the fun bachelor) and I need those bills for the trip (woman with the soda crackers)."

"Short on cash?" the waiter said.

"I'll give you the rest next week," my date said.

I've been a waiter. "Coming back next week" to leave a tip doesn't cut it. I was afraid to look our ponytailed Paul in the eye. How could a wonderful evening have gone so disastrously wrong? Although some of my other paramours had done things like shatter all my dreams, they would never have stiffed Paul.

Unrefrigerated wanted to go to Starbucks afterward and read the latest issue of *Seattle Magazine*.

"They're featuring cheap places to eat," he said. "We can find some more restaurants to go to."

"Do you want dessert or anything?" he said as we waited for our coffees at the counter.

"Well, no, if you don't have any cash."

"It's okay," he assured me. "I can just break a hundred."

BUNK DEBUNK

Myth: Men Always Come Back.

Bunked!

It may be wishful thinking on my part—I prefer to think no man could ever, ever forget me—but I think it's pretty rare that a man you've dated more than a few times disappears completely . . . of course whatever made you stop seeing each other probably hasn't disappeared completely either, unfortunately.

DATE 20 Coffee Date of Sorrow, Coffee Date of Pain

TRUE CONFESSION

This same guy wrote to me every time I did a week-long free trial of Matchmaker.com and did not remember me each time. This was the first time things progressed to meeting in person.

I couldn't believe I was back to online dating, but once I resigned myself to it I did it with a vengeance. I put up a picture that showed off my body and made me look a lot more fun than I am willing to be on a first date.

I registered for a free week-long trial on Matchmaker.com and tossed out a few snappy answers to their form questions. I even put in a sort of disclaimer that I write about my love life and if a man dates me he may end up on TV. I'm sure that will protect me from lawsuits in the future.

My inbox reached its limit of fifty letters in no time. E-mails like "Ouch!!! Your picture is hot" were just the boost my flagging ego needed. As I sorted through the spelling errors, sexual come-ons, and form letters that commented on things not even listed in my profile, it made me see what a rich and untapped pool of men there are out there, among them a nudist, a surfer named Kid Kandy who listed his pet peeve as "chicks that won't go down," and a guy from Iceland. The questionnaire asked people to list their likes and dislikes. One guy said he enjoys dropping acid before job interviews, telling kids there's no Santa Claus, and leading car salesmen to believe he's actually interested in buying a car.

Internet dating has a bloodless efficiency that is perfect for me. I was running a complex dating assembly line that was broken down into different stages. While I was getting ready to go out and meet one date, I was e-mailing new recruits and booking times with others. It was not a wacky, *I Love Lucy*–type system, but something with a crisp sense of purpose that the military would envy.

When you try online dating a few different times over the course of a year or two, there will always be a few guys who write to you each time . . . and don't remember you each time. They are men who've made a career out of Matchmaker.com, either because they're undesirables and can't find anyone, or they're too desirable and know they can have anyone. That night I had a date with someone I was pretty sure was one of the latter.

He said he was a journalist and the picture in his online profile was that of a cocky cub reporter. I felt uncharacteristically nervous about whether or not he would like me.

He suggested a great Irish bar downtown. The weather was sunny, so I decided to walk there. It was early May, and spring, tentative at first, had burst into a symphony of sidewalk life: dreadlocked teenagers were chatting and sitting cross-legged on the pavement, a couple on the patio of a streetside café were smoking and picking the sweet meat out of oysters doused in red sauce. A group was going through the ritual of figuring out who owed how much of the bill before wandering off to a Mariners game.

I saw a lone man sitting outside the pub in a worn-in leather jacket. I knew it was him. He was much older than his picture, but he also looked a lot better. The years had agreed with him.

We introduced ourselves and he said the bar was too crowded and that we could go to the Starbucks down the block. I was being subjected to the First-Date Downgrade, a hazard I should have been looking for knowing I was out with a career online dater. I had really been looking forward to having a drink, too. As we were getting up to leave the waitress brought two black, frosty pints of Guinness to the table next to us. I almost asked them if I could just have a sip.

Men are gutsy. If I had offered something good, let's say a blow job, and then bait and switched to something shitty, let's say watching *Beaches*, would a man just smile and go along with the plan? Would I make him go through with it when I saw that he was unhappy? Doubtful.

Being a woman I made the best of it. I held my head high as I entered the empty Starbucks and ordered my usual, a tall drip. I wondered if I was with one. He paid (let's hope) and we sat outside. I'm always a little uncomfortable on coffee dates and never more so than when they take place at dinnertime. At one point I had my legs crossed so hard I think I pulled one of my quadriceps.

Things picked up with the conversation. He's a muckraker for a free paper, Sinclair Lewis with 1-800 girls on the back pages, but still. He is apparently well respected for his work and I found it quite glamorous: lawsuits, death threats, low pay. Some people have all the luck.

We talked about baby boomers: sellouts, and California: friendlier and flakier than the Pacific Northwest. He told me about a lunch date where the woman he was seeing had screamed and thrown things at him. When men announce that they have dated a drama queen, I'm usually suspicious of them rather than the woman. For one thing, they picked her and for another, even if she's crazy, they may have driven her there. As we parted ways after about two hours, he thanked me for making him feel so comfortable and it occurred to me that he had mostly just used me as a sounding board.

When I got home I looked up articles he had written on the Internet and saw that he is as well known for his depression as he is for his investigative skills. My first thought was to write the date up as a parody of *The Bell Jar*, which felt disingenuous since I haven't read it. Then I considered spoofing something by Tennessee Williams. I very much enjoyed *Cat on a Hot Tin Roof* with Paul Newman and Elizabeth Taylor, but that didn't quite fit either. In the end I settled on a plain, straight write-up of him as a professional dater, because I felt too guilty doing otherwise.

I called him Broken to describe the worn-in quality of the leather jacket he was wearing, but it ironically described his psyche. What is it about depression that makes it a sacred cow to someone like me? If a nondepressed man downgraded a date and then proceeded to use a strange woman as his therapist, he would be considered a self-absorbed asshole, but if a depressed man does those things and then shrouds himself in sackcloth and ashes, or in his case banner headlines, he's somehow brave and noble. Admitting to depression is a shield to ward off any possible criticism from a disappointed woman. How could one be cold enough to complain about a walking male-confessional novel, after all?

I felt that Broken was smart enough to know all of this, but I still played along.

I wondered how it would be if the situation were reversed. If I were depressed and telling a stranger from the Internet about my dating problems, would he feel compassion for me? Or would he just tell his buddies: "Chick was a drag, man. I didn't even get a blow job"?

Or maybe he would naturally cut me more slack than a happy man; maybe Broken would be kinder and more emotionally rich than the regular guys I've dated.

I never did find out.

"Thanks for making me feel so comfortable," he had said, probably already knowing he was never going to call again.

Just as well. I find Starbucks at dinnertime depressing.

BUNK DEBUNK

Myth: His exes were all psychos, so of course the relationships were bad. He'll be different with me.

Debunked!

This statement has more red flags than a May Day parade in China. First of all, when someone describes most of his exes as crazy, he is either (1) lying, (2) seeking out that type, or (3) has driven them there. I'm sure there is a better measure of a person's relationship behavior than his past, but I'll be hog-tied if I can come up with it, Jethro. Unless you want That Psycho [state your name] I Used to Date to be the way you're referred to at parties in the future, I'd steer clear.

DATE 21 Didja Hear the One About the Unfunny Comedian?

TRUE CONFESSION

At forty-seven, he turned out to be the oldest of all my dates. I made a joke that after my catastrophe with the playboy-snowboarder, Christmas Tree, I had gone "from a hipster to a hip replacement." Then I felt mean and stopped saying that.

It was a Sunday morning and the heavens had opened up to dump buckets of lemon yellow sunshine on the unsuspecting people below. I had two dates that day. The first was brunch with a middle-aged comedian who was originally from Los Angeles. He was waiting outside and we liked each other right away. He had thoughtfully made reservations. I felt like a rock star as the host whisked us past all the losers who hadn't put their names on the list. We got a cozy corner table by the window and he told me about his act, in fact part of the time I think he was doing his act.

Who did he remind me of? Who did he remind me of? It was driving me nuts. Someone older and famous. Someone on TV, I thought.

He had been in at least one movie, but had mostly worked as an instructor at comedy traffic school. For the uninitiated, that's eight hours of stand-up and road rules for a captive audience. He confided that it was a great way to meet women, as students would approach him after the class and there was no conflict of interest on his part since he wasn't a real professor and they weren't real students.

I'm in awe of women who can ask men out. If I were a man I would be a virgin. Actually, I tell myself if I were a man I would just be Johnny Depp. Since it's hypothetical, why not?

On the Matchmaker.com questionnaire they ask you where you would be willing to meet someone in person. He told me about one woman he met who answered that she would only consider meeting a man in a pubic area. She got hundreds of responses to her ad. I laughed. Later when I thought of it, it seemed like a dating urban legend, though.

I had already eaten since I am confused about whether a guy is asking me to a meal or if it's some red herring and we will end up at Starbucks. I ordered a parfait of honey yogurt, granola, and fresh pineapple and strawberries. The Pretty Parfait.

"It's called pretty and you're pretty," the Comedian giggled. Who did he remind me of? It was someone else who giggles.

He had the more manly breakfast I would normally choose: eggs and meat and hash browns with catsup. Red flannel eggs.

He said he didn't mind being written about but that I might end up in his comedy act. Since every other Tuesday at Huey's Ha-Ha Haven isn't exactly the fast track, I said I didn't care.

As I was walking home I realized who he had reminded me of: the Pillsbury Doughboy.

BUNK DEBUNK

Myth: In time you'll forget all about him.

Debunked!

I don't know if it's because I have too many planets in Scorpio or that I didn't get enough attention as a child (not likely, since I successfully talked both my siblings into moving out of the house by the time I was seven), but I go through phases of being sick with jealousy over guys from my past.

Since most of my former flames work in the arts, they're very easy to check up on. There is always an article being written or an old interview I may not have seen yet. A corollary to the problem of having exes bordering on the public eye is that they sometimes tend to move on to women who are also bordering there with them.

There I am minding my own business, innocently advance-searching the Internet for any scrap of information about an ex, and some film reviewer is hitting me over the head with the news that he's dating an actress. After I've seen one of her two films—usually a midnight-movie soft-core, I didn't date Scorsese, after all—I have the urge to just call him. Who cares that it was me who blew him off or that we haven't talked in years or that I don't have his phone number. I will just throw myself on his mercy, pride be damned, and we will get this whole him-having-a-life-after-me silliness straightened out.

While I would like to picture an exchange worthy of Cary Grant and Katharine Hepburn, complete with cigarettes and martinis, I'm afraid the conversation would be more like:

Me: I saw your girlfriend's latest film. She looks like a man and she can't act.

Him: She has a beautiful face . . .

Me: If by *beautiful face* you mean *like Tom Petty's*, then, yes . . .

Him: . . . and does incredible acting . . .

Me: Sure, if by *incredible acting* you mean *like Tom Petty's*.

It's not wholly fair on my part. I thought he was pretty good in that video where he plays the Mad Hatter, for instance, but you get the picture.

Seeing my ex's current girlfriend tilts my perspective like a pinball machine. In the world in my head, my old boyfriends mourn for a suitable three to five years and then eventually move on to Catherine Zeta-Jones duplicates who scored higher on the Mensa test than I did. It is also a world in which I am considered sane, ambitious, and good at planning things.

The other day when I was in full ex obsession, I stumbled upon an interview where he actually mentioned the woman he is dating. It must be serious. And by that I mean she must be prettier than me.

My problem—besides the fact that my life was clearly over—was that I didn't have plans until that evening and I needed to kill a few hours before seeing friends.

I spent the day thinking up other topics of conversation for that night. Things that wouldn't indicate how really twisted and needy I am. I knew I'd be fine once I met up with everyone at the bowling alley; it was the ride there I was most concerned with. A woman named Marilyn, who I didn't know really well, was picking me up. She was bright and together and stable: things I've read about but never actually experienced.

We ran out of the small talk I had planned—what's your favorite vegetable, how do *you* feel about yarn—a few blocks from my house and lapsed into a quick, not uncomfortable silence.

"Do you ever wonder so much about an ex that you almost can't make it through the day?" she asked, squinting into the early evening sun as we curved onto the I-5. "I tell ya, I'd pay good money to find out what every one of my exes is doing. If he got married and if he has deep regrets that we didn't work out."

I was surprised to hear it from someone who's happily married and admits her exes weren't that great. I spilled my whole story in one run-on sentence. My goal was to not bring up my obsession, not keep quiet if someone else did.

I didn't bring it up again at dinner.

We were at a little Italian place in the university district with plastic checkered tablecloths and red wine served in water glasses. It was 1:00 a.m.

". . . because it's just the kind of thing a normal person would mention. I'll see you at home." Kate finished up a quick cell phone call from her boyfriend.

"He and his ex are still friends, which is fine," she explained. "But he was getting a haircut from her the other night and when I went to pick him up she answered the door with a pair of scissors and nothing else. Apparently she's a nudist and he 'forgot' to tell me."

"Exes! I was fixated on meeting his," said Sonja—blonde, Swedish, former model Sonja—pointing at her husband's back. "I got my chance when we were invited to the same wedding. It was really bad because he and I were on vacation in Canada and we left early so I could see her. He wanted to spend our last afternoon at the pool, but I said, 'We have to leave now!' (tapping her watch). 'I packed your bag for you. Chop-chop!'

"We got there and I thought someone had invited Michelle Pfeiffer. She was absolutely beautiful. I couldn't even look at the bride during the ceremony. I don't know why he didn't tell me how stunning she is. What kind of a man doesn't go on and on to his wife about how beautiful his former girlfriend is?"

Either it's wholly sane and healthy to have a poison-spewing green-eyed creature lurking just below the surface of what appears to be a well-adjusted female or I've found a group of women to whom I can really relate.

When we left the restaurant, a fine mist had shellacked the street. Knowing that other people carried feelings about past loves and even about *their* past loves didn't dull my own regrets any more than the years had, though. I still wish I had said I was sorry before it was too late or at least before I had left Los Angeles.

It's the kind of thing a normal person would mention.

DATE 22 When Immigration Smiles at Me, I Go to Rio

TRUE CONFESSION

I felt like Sophia Loren/Grace Kelly dashing from breakfast with an L.A. gentleman who's been in pictures to a late lunch with a Brazilian stranger. Except for the woman sitting behind me on the #15 bus muttering, "Have you found Jesus yet?" and pulling out strands of my hair, it was just like being in a Cary Grant movie.

Later that day I went to Pike Place Market for my second date. It was another blind date from the Internet, this time with a man from Rio.

We met outside of a restaurant and he asked me to walk with him along the water. He was dark with a goofy smile and probably about my height. It felt strange to just be walking with no plans, but his beautiful lilting Brazilian accent swept me in.

"After a year and a half in this country I don't feel like a fish out of water anymore. I have finally found my aquarium."

We walked into the crowded market area past flower stalls selling huge bouquets of tulips and irises and daisies.

"Americans are so closed. You're afraid of letting others into your little individual worlds. I wish you were all more like Michael Moore."

111

"Invasive fat men with cameras and poor boundaries?"

He laughed.

"I'm teasing. I love Michael Moore."

Like most foreigners in Seattle, he worked for Microsoft. As we passed the famous fishmongers throwing halibut to an electrical storm of tourists' flashbulbs, Rio told me that his company uses the fish guys' training videos to inspire employees. That could explain some of the problems with Word, since I'm not sure peripherals and halibut are interchangeable.

I had forgotten that I wrote in my ad that a guy may end up getting written about if he dates me.

"I'm trying to say interesting things so I can end up in a book someday. Do you have a Web site or anything?"

"No," I lied. I was having a nice day and didn't want to spoil it by talking about my version of work. Or by being truthful.

We were past the market and he stopped me at the corner.

"Your picture on the dating site caught my eye, all that life in you. Hundreds of people pass by you every day and only a few stand out in color. You are one of those few. Do me the honor of joining me for a meal and a drink."

We walked down the alley to the restaurant with the pink décor and huge patio overlooking the water. I ordered a pink mojito to go with the color scheme and we agreed to split an antipasto appetizer with prosciutto, white beans, mozzarella cheese, olives, hot peppers, salad in vinaigrette, beets, and mango.

"When we met I wanted to give you a kiss on each cheek as they do in my country. I felt embarrassed to, though. Sensuality is a part of Brazilian culture, but it's not like that here."

"Maybe it's because G-strings and public toplessness are not a part of the culture here," I said.

He asked if I'd ever been married and I said no. I asked if he ever had and he took a too-long pause. I asked if he was still married and he said no. I asked if it happened in this country and he said yes.

"How could you be married and divorced within a year and a half?"

"I've been here three years."

"That's a different time line from the one you gave an hour ago."

"You're so American."

"What happened with your marriage?"

"She was not my Cinderella and I was not her Prince Charming, but sometimes you're so abandoned and alone that all someone has to do is run her fingers through your hair and you fall in love. Plus I needed a green card. What's your fairy tale?"

Rumpelstiltskin, with me as the chick spinning stories of gold and attracting strange men in return? Red Riding Hood with men as the Wolf? No, I'm too old to attract pedophiles. The Snow Queen? Probably too majestic and regal, plus I'm not sure how it ends. Sleeping Beauty being woken with a kiss seems to ascribe way too much power to the prince's ability to give a decent orgasm, although maybe I'll back-burner that one.

"I think maybe Cinderella is my story, too," I said.

The flouncing maître d' must have seen some look on my face because he mouthed, "Do you need your check?" to me. Gay men have a sixth sense about these things and only they and French guys should be allowed to be hosts.

As we left the restaurant, Rio mentioned that he shared a house with someone. His wife, maybe?

He kissed me on both cheeks as he had said he wanted to when we met and I never saw him again.

BUNK DEBUNK

Myth: Men and women have different attitudes toward casual sex.

Bunked! (well, obviously)

I was innocently browsing a Chicago community board to see how I could get my writing on National Public Radio's *This American Life* when I noticed a heated debate about the hottest of topics: the difference between how men and women regard sex.

A guy was lamenting the lack of women who place ads looking for casual encounters. He said that a woman looking for no-strings sex is a hot commodity, while a man looking for the same is viewed as pathetic and horny. He then went on to argue that this imbalance gives women the upper hand in relationships.

A woman responded that for him to say that women have the upper hand because of the availability of something they don't want anyway is ludicrous. That it's like saying that men have the upper hand in looking for long-term emotional intimacy and commitment, no sex required.

Another woman had a ballsier take. She said that she is now married, but for ten years she partied like Mick Jagger and learned a few things about men in the process.

Lesson #1: The easiest way to get a man to call after sex is to not care if he calls.

Lesson #2: The easiest way to get a man to be faithful is to tell him you do not believe in monogamy.

I do think it's human nature to want what you can't have, and I know from my own aversion to intimacy that if you distance yourself from a man, he will press you with questions about where the relationship is going.

Although I'm not afraid of artistic risks, I'm scared to death of relationship risks. I'm not Mick Jagger. I'm not even one of those guys from Weezer. I'm too chicken to see what would happen if I tried to have sex like a man. I would love to experiment and write about it, but I would care too much about the guy, I know it.

I think it's less how you approach sex than how you feel about it afterward that really separates men and women, anyway.

DATE 23 Lunch, Mouse, Good.

TRUE CONFESSION

I adore Mouse but I suspect we may be each other's near miss (and near mister).

I woke up with a slight cold and hair like Elaine's from *Seinfeld*. It crossed my mind to cancel my date, but I had plans to meet the Mouse King at the pig statue in Pike Market and I really wanted to see him. I took some Alka-Seltzer Plus cold medicine, put my hair up in a series of clips and braids, and ventured out into the fine mist. There are days in Seattle that defeat even the most high-powered straightening iron and this was one of them.

I saw that I was early, so I sat down on the curb and put a dust of pale powder on my face and a slick of matte rose lipstick and Vaseline on my lips. A mother ordered her screaming child to "sit on that pig and I don't care if you don't like it, I want to take a picture." I noticed that the pig is not an unusual meeting place. A man greeted a woman with a kiss, people came alone and left together.

Mouse arrived and gave me a hug. "I wasn't sure you were coming, but I thought I'd show up just in case."

"I called you back to say I'd be here," I said.

"I didn't get a message." He sounded like he didn't believe me. "Oh well, it's nice to see you." Sometimes I don't understand male logic. If I were going to lie, it would be about something worthwhile like my age. Why would I lie about anything as mundane as a phone call when it's so easy to dispute?

He took me to a second-story Bolivian place with a patio and a great view looking down at the market crowd. I took the seat facing the mountains; Mouse took the seat facing a guy with a parrot on his shoulder.

"How would you feel if a guy showed up for a date wearing a bird?"

"As a writer desperate for material, I only wish someone would."

Mouse knows all the great hideaways in the market. It's one of my favorite things about him. I feel that knowing which restaurants to go to (not necessarily the expensive ones, but the ones with character) is as good a measure of a man as any. I had never even noticed this place before.

"Do you eat at the market often?" I asked.

"I was here for drinks with a woman the other night. Our mothers are friends and set us up."

"Did you buy her a book as a gift too?" I asked, thinking of the writing book he'd given me on our first date.

"I didn't know enough about her to buy her a book. I told her I dated you, though."

"Now why would that be any sort of recommendation to a woman?"

He had some chicken, onions, and peppers over rice and I had spicy shrimp soup. Both came with a simple salad with lettuce, onions, and a vinegar dressing.

I said that when I go out with a guy who's over thirty-five and wants to be married but never has been, I can usually see why. Mouse said, "What about women who haven't been married?" and eyed me accusingly. I explained that it's different for women because they have to wait to be chosen, but if a man wants to get married he can pretty much just ask someone. Mouse got offended and made me stop talking, which seemed oversensitive as he wasn't even thirty yet.

I think marriage is to men what sex is to women. Most women can pretty much just pick up the phone and get free delivery from any number of men if sex is all they want. If a decent guy wants to get married and doesn't have a lot of fairy-tale ideals about relationships, I would argue that he can do the same, with a slightly longer time frame to allow for hiring a caterer and a band.

One of the things I like about Mouse is that he knows about the Web site. I can talk about my work problems with him.

"I've been feeling tormented lately because most of the men I've written about don't really know I write about them," I said.

"A friend of mine saw your site and he said he wishes women would review his dates. At least then he'd know what he's doing wrong."

I turned my face up to the sky. "The sun feels good."

"In Seattle the opportunity for love increases in direct proportion to the number of sunny days—as the weather gets nicer, the hookups get more frequent," he said.

"In Minneapolis, where I'm from, people know they need to find someone around November, or it will be a long and lonely winter—not too many opportunities to 'show your wares' if you're bundled up in a parka. When spring comes, everyone breaks up, suddenly free from concealing clothing and questionable late-fall romantic choices."

"Since the weather here isn't as extreme, neither is the courtship. During the rainy season, people just get depressed and watch more TV," he said.

It had been dreary ever since I started my Web site. I was interested to see if seasonal changes brought me personal changes.

Since the common lore is that summer in Seattle doesn't start until after the Fourth of July, I found little comfort.

After lunch Mouse took me to a cool bakery known for desserts made with coconut and cream. He got the stink eye from the guy in line ahead of us because he was propping open the door with his body and letting in the cool air. He apologized, which I thought was gracious, since it's pretty much the norm to have the door open in a popular place that fits three patrons when there are ten people waiting.

He bought a bag of tasty little coconut cookies and gave me one.

"Stick with me, kid. I know all the little hideaways."

I knew then that he hadn't read about my tryst with Christmas Tree yet.

Later that day I got an e-mail from him that said: "I checked your site when I got back to work after our lunch. We're friends, you can talk to me about anything . . . including irresponsible guys."

BUNK DEBUNK

Myth: Never-married men over thirty-five are bad news. (Part I)

Bunked!

Of course I'm just talking about if you want a commitment from them, not that they're bad news in general. I mean clearly they're not all criminals or anything. Well, some of them may be, but that's not what I meant at all. I have gotten in so much trouble for saying this, especially since I'm over thirty-five and a never-married myself. It's just that, *in general,* women want a long-term commitment and, *in general*, it's men who ask for that commitment. If a desirable guy has managed to escape the noose, or rather has not met the exact right lady of his dreams yet, he may not be so easy to snare/connect with on the deep soul mate–type level for which he is clearly holding out.

DATE 24 Lunch, Mouse, Bad.

TRUE CONFESSION

I've developed a theory that the people who succeed in the arts are those who have mates that are in denial right along with them. "Darling, of course you're going to make it despite your financial situation, your latest reviews, and the advice of every *not* insane person you know stating the contrary."

When I was seventeen, my best girl friend came to school one morning with a Band-Aid all along the length of her shin. She explained that she had shaved off a swath of skin along with her leg hair the night before.

"I realized the razor had caught the skin near my ankle, and I don't know why, but I just kept dragging it up to my knee."

Unlike flash floods or a stray cigarette sending a dry field into flames, sometimes we know things are off, we can see them happening because they're slow paced, it's completely within our power to stop them, and yet we don't. It's as if we have a voice inside us that can't read a map encouraging us to keep going in what we know is the wrong direction using the logic, "Let's see where this takes us!" as we steer the car into the nearest lake, all the while minding the speed limit. Given a choice between the mentally challenged passenger chirping out wrong directions or the driver who listens to them, who's the real idiot in this scenario, though?

121

My first clue that things were headed in the wrong direction with Mouse was that we were going on a lunch date that neither of us had asked for. His cell phone had malfunctioned and he had just gotten the voice mail that he didn't believe I sent from our date last week. The message said that I was running a few minutes late and that I was looking forward to seeing him. He mistook it for me wanting to meet that day, and although I didn't know what he was talking about, we agreed to have lunch at a diner. Our date was a passionless arranged marriage, with an errant cell phone standing in for the desperate, exhausted parents.

Sensing my frustration with my writing career, Mouse told me with no hint of sarcasm that I should become a ski instructor. He was the second person in as many weeks to suggest this, which was really bad, since for one thing I was not asking for career advice and for another I do not ski.

He went on to observe that "this writing thing doesn't seem to be working out for you." I searched his face for a clue that he was just teasing as he said supportive things like "You've been at this for a long time and I don't see it going anywhere."

I ordered a Reuben and had the waiter substitute turkey for the corned beef. In a daring menu choice they don't serve French fries at this particular diner and the Swiss cheese from my sandwich had melted and hardened into my potato chips.

Mouse could tell that maybe he had said the wrong thing after I gave one-word answers for twenty minutes, so he tried to distract me by pointing out colorful artwork on the walls that was done by fourth graders from the Catholic school around the corner. I noticed that a few of the children were still painting at the third-grade level. I'm sure they will have brilliant careers as writers-cum-ski-instructors someday.

Some sort of unholy compulsion made me return to the subject of my career.

"What did you think of 'Maureen and the Seniors'?" He had

been one of the few people to whom I had sent a recent short story about my girl friend's experience with volunteering at a downtown senior center. I thought it was my best work to date and felt vulnerable about it.

"I probably shouldn't criticize you so much, but . . . oh hell, you get criticized all the time," he said. "I liked the part where you said the senior center wasn't 'a gentle, lavender-scented world of Ruths and Ediths, but was rather a tough, chain-smoking world of Summers and Cats' and I liked the part where one of the Summers got suspended from bingo for two weeks for starting a fistfight, but why would only one woman sign up to go to the art gallery at the end?"

"I guess because they were all so bored by Maureen's first outing that word got around and no one else signed up for the second one."

"But that doesn't make any sense."

"It's what really happened, though."

"Your job as a writer is to make a good story, not to say what really happens."

At least we were back to referring to writing and not skiing as my job.

One of my biggest fears about marriage is that a man will erode my optimism with his negative, hopeless version of my reality until it becomes my own. A car trundling toward a career or a life neither of us consciously chose, power windows locked, foot lightly but steadily on the gas pedal.

Although I never dated him again, Mouse did not drive us into the nearest lake or to the nearest ski resort. Instead he drove me home with the radio tuned to a station that had been interested in making my writing a regular feature at one time until they decided to go in a different direction.

DATE 25 Didja Hear the One About the Movie Star and the Midget?

TRUE CONFESSION

Sometimes I miss the complete absurdity of dating in Los Angeles: C-list actors, middle-aged men with pretty nymphets, fake blood . . . Thank God Seattle is only an hour and a half or, in this case, a dinner date away.

"How come you never scream when we have sex?" my date said.

"Give me something to scream about," his girlfriend answered. I watched as their witty repartee was interrupted by a man in a white mask who eviscerated my date, hung him in a deer shed, and later made him into spiced sausages to sell at a roadside stand to horny, unsuspecting teenagers on their way to Lake Badajuju.

The Comedian had had a pivotal role in a mediocre sequel of an extremely successful slasher franchise in the '80s and I had rented the DVD in the name of research.

Beheadings, electrocutions, and an unusually high number of unexplained ax murders—it had a high attrition rate for a resort area. Yet every summer nubile young people returned to investigate scratching noises in the basement, take wooden boats out on the water late at night, and frolic naked with their attractive, equally unforesightful friends.

We had planned on having a Sunday picnic, but the weather was a typical shade of Seattle gray, so we had dinner at a restaurant on the water instead. I knew it was silly but I was relieved that we wouldn't be going to a lake.

I like to correct for my bad dating choices by going for someone completely different from the last guys I dated, which in this case were younger men, one of whom had interests that included snowboarding and seeing other women naked. I was pleased to meet the Comedian because he is older and more mature than the snowboarder. He is also older and more mature than me. Honestly, he is older and more mature than Johnny Cash when he was into his third decade of performing, and he is currently pricing hip replacements, but he is polite and he picks up the check.

The Polynesian-Japanese restaurant he took me to was one part kitsch, one part best meal I've had in ages. He hadn't made reservations, so we waited for a table at the bar and drank hot sake.

The restaurant was filled with paper fish, pink Lava lamps oozing glitter, and the kind of beautiful young people one might find in a horror film. We were seated at a cozy booth and the Comedian ordered chicken skewers, jumbo prawns with coconut, and a tempura platter with vegetables and shrimp for us to share. They all had dipping sauces.

He told me about his latest comedy routine. One thing that apparently had gotten a big laugh last weekend was when he said that while he's making conversation with a woman on a date, he's really thinking "I wonder what she looks like bent over."

I was really thinking, *I wonder why I'm with someone with no social skills*.

I think he could tell he wasn't making progress with me because he asked me what my type is. I don't think I have a type, but I have types of things I don't like and this not-so-subtle sexual testing is one of them.

After we had eaten, we headed to the door and there was a sudden deluge happening outside. He ran to the car and got an umbrella so my leather jacket wouldn't be ruined. He wanted to kiss me in the car. I swear I'm not uptight, though I am often called so. "I like to get to know someone for about six months before I get physical," I said. "What do you think?"

"I think that women overthink these things. I saw a movie once where a woman fell for a guy who said, 'Open your mind and your legs will follow.'"

"I saw a movie once where a guy was handsome and charming and didn't say weird things. I think it starred Kevin Bacon."

"When did you first realize that you hate men?" he said.

I figured that would be the end of the date, but he wanted to see a movie.

We considered *Identity*, which was reviewed as a slasher film, but also confusingly starred John Cusack. Turns out it was a slasher film that starred John Cusack. There was a twist at the end, but that didn't decrease the number of bodies stacking up during the first hour and forty-five minutes. During the filming of the slasher movie he was in, the Comedian managed to handle being dismembered by a man in a white sports mask for an entire six weeks; watching this movie with me he jumped and squealed like an eleven-year-old girl every time someone on the screen got chopped up, which was every ten minutes. I hardly jumped at all, numbed from all the sake.

On the way home, he told me about the time he met one of his boyhood fantasies, Julie Newmar, who played Catwoman in the *Batman* television show. He walked right up to her and said, "I heard a rumor about you and a midget." Julie Newmar is five foot eleven. The story went that a midget approached her at a party and said, "I was wondering if I could have sex with you?" She was supposed to have answered, "If you do, and I hear about it . . ."

Did rejecting the advances of a little person mean that Julie

Newmar also hated men or was it just a problem of logistics in her case?

"When did you first realize that you hate men?" I couldn't get his words out of my head. Was I a silent, relentless predator, hacking up men's feelings and slashing apart my own chances at love?

I think perhaps it was more that certain men hate not getting their way and it's easier to blame it on man-hating women than to accept that maybe a woman doesn't want to have sex with them in particular. Mouse was hating me for choosing Christmas Tree, why else the unprovoked ski instructor comments at the diner? The Comedian was hating me for not being attracted to him, why else the raunchy dinner conversation?

Maybe there was a reason that sex and hacked-up bodies were so closely related in slasher films—the monstrous killing machines probably just felt bad about being left out. They were the only ones in the film not having enthusiastic romps in hammocks, tents, cars, and on the floating dock, after all.

After he dropped me off, I ran from the Comedian's car to my apartment building in the pouring rain. I walked up the dark staircase to my apartment. The lone fluorescent light in the hallway flickered, threatening to go out, and I heard the rain beating down on the roof.

That night in my dreams, against our better judgment, Catwoman and I ran up the stairs of an old house. The lights had gone out due to the storm. We locked the bedroom door behind us, gasping for air, while on the other side Billy Barty and the Pillsbury Doughboy rhythmically threw their weight against it over and over and over.

BUNK DEBUNK

Myth: Never-married men over thirty-five are bad news. (Part II)

Bunked!

Look, I'm just saying that generally it's the men who are the choosers and the women who are the chosen, so if a man isn't married by thirty-five—late thirties tops and that's the highest I'll go, I mean it—it says something about his desire to be coupled off. Sure, there could be extenuating circumstances like his fiancée died or left him. That's good news! Not for her if she died, obviously, but for you if you're dating him.

DATE 26 You Yell "Date!" and We've Got a Panic on Our Hands

TRUE CONFESSION

This was the first singles event I had ever attended in my life. I felt horribly conspicuous even though I had brought a date. Then I ended up actually being conspicuous *because* of my date.

I got a last-minute invitation to an event being thrown by my friend Anastasia.

She and her boyfriend were hosting a dinner-and-a-movie night at the Jimi Hendrix museum. They serve a meal that goes with the theme of a movie. For instance, two weeks ago the movie was *Clerks*, which is set in a convenience store in Jersey, so the entrée was burgers left under heat lamps for a really long time and stale Kit Kats for dessert. On the menu this time: *Jaws*. "Bring Comedy Boy or whatever you call him," Anastasia's boyfriend said. The Comedian was audibly surprised that I called him, as it was so obvious that things hadn't gone that well on our last date.

Since our dinner was complimentary, we were seated at the reviewers' table, a nice way of saying Table for Those Who Couldn't Get a Date. Our dinner companions were Nick, a quadriplegic software engineer; Marty, a Harley rider who stood four foot eleven in cowboy boots; and Chris, a quiet guy with occasional outbursts due to Tourette's.

After a half hour and a glass of chardonnay, Nick was telling me about commuting to Redmond in a special car, Marty was saying it doesn't matter how tall you are when you're on a hog, and Chris was telling a lively story about his trip to England with only a few misplaced expletives.

Marty and I got into a nice conversation about rock and roll—he quoted Homer Simpson that "we haven't heard the last of Dexy's Midnight Runners." He told me he met Clapton, Townshend, Page, and Di Meola when he accidentally wandered backstage at a concert once when he was sixteen.

Seeing me distracted by an interesting conversation, my date quickly established himself as the most handicapped person at the table. What I had been mistaking for manners was apparently just lack of an audience.

Jokes that started with "Have you heard the one about the movie star and the midget extra . . ." were unfortunately accompanied by pantomime. I could barely eat my halibut with a chicken leg sticking out of its mouth doused in catsup because the Comedian was telling an anal sex joke and the table was vibrating.

After dinner I ate an entire container of herbed gourmet popcorn, two Reese's peanut butter cups, and the cotton-candy hair off a Little Richard sundae given to us by another table. Then I excused myself to the ladies' room. When I got back my date was frantically trying to flirt with Anastasia, despite the fact that she was too young for him, too gorgeous for him, and had a boyfriend standing twenty feet away.

I left him alone for five minutes and he was humping her leg like a pug. I said hello to the two of them and he shooed me away by saying, "Don't forget your sweater in the other room." I can only imagine what transpired while I fetched my cardigan. I would have to send an apology note on Monday.

In Spielberg's film a vicious two-thousand-pound creature with prehistoric instincts rips innocent swimmers limb from limb. As my date probed in the dark for the half a Butterfinger he had dropped in my lap, I was beginning to envy them.

BUNK DEBUNK

Myth: *The third date is the "sex date."*

Debunked!

Not according to most of the guys who date me! But seriously, the fact that I can't get a consensus on this tells me that there is no rule. It's my personal belief that the people who have sex on the first date balance out the people who think they're going to hell if they have sex before marriage (and give in after like ten dates), to create a third-date average for everyone.

DATE 27   The $40 Bottle of Wine

TRUE CONFESSION

At twenty-six, he was not only the youngest guy I dated but, I later told girl friends, the only guy I would have considered marrying. Within the past six months anyway. Devastating.

Jimi Hendrix's purple velvet coat is hanging downstairs and my black leather one is hanging over my arm. The party is packed. I'm talking to Anastasia, rather I'm listening to her talking to some guy who's trying to sell her on his graphic-design ideas—she needs a logo for her party business and I need something to happen. I'm bored. Parties at the Hendrix museum are a great idea in theory, but the reality is that the bar is as sterile as one you'd find in an airport. Now if we were all drinking and canoodling among the display cases, then yeah. Quite likely the men from Anastasia's social club would do better working on chicks surrounded by Nirvana's drum sticks and Pearl Jam's guitars . . . or maybe not with the regular guy vs. rock star comparison factor and all.

"This is the lady you need to know in Seattle." Two blondish guys came over, one smaller and cute with straight hair, the other one taller and cute with curly hair. The smaller one introduced them. My interest level was still low—everyone's always approaching Anastasia, since she really is the person to know in Seattle if you're single.

"I'm from Memphis," the smaller one said, apparently trying to include me in the conversation, judging by his eye contact.

"Elvis." I nodded.

"Yeah, I've dressed as him for Halloween. I did well with that, actually."

"You remind me of Rob Lowe," I said. I was referring to his voice.

"People usually say Tobey Maguire . . . or Dumbo."

"Your ears do stick out a little," I said. "You don't seem old enough to be here."

"I'm almost twenty-seven, I just dress like I'm twelve." He was wearing a striped cotton top that did look a little young, now that he mentioned it. "I'm turning twenty-seven next week and I'm already retired."

"Really, from what?" My interest level was going way up. He was either witty or wealthy or both.

"I'm a lawyer," he said. "I did really well with it, but I didn't like it, so I quit."

"I'm retired, too," I said. "Well, unemployed, really. I have a job interview next week but I don't know what to wear."

"How are your legs? That's the only question mark, since you're wearing pants. The rest of you is definitely marketable."

Anastasia and the curly-haired blond guy had long since lost interest in us and left.

We walked to the bar and he bought us each another drink. I was flattered. Rob Lowe Voice was a cute, younger guy who not only could afford to stop working, but, I soon found out, could afford to own in my neighborhood. Impossible.

"I'm programming you into my phone right now and we're going out tomorrow night. I would ask you out for Saturday night, but that's too serious for us this early in our relationship," he said.

"That cocktail waitress is the most beautiful woman in the room," I said. "Maybe you can ask her out for Saturday night."

"No, I couldn't! My confidence level would have to be one hundred percent to get a waitress. They get hit on all the time."

We made plans to have a drink the next night at a wine bar near my apartment. I left the party soon after and slipped out the back door of the museum. The cocktail waitress I had alluded to earlier was sitting on a cement parking divider smoking a cigarette. Men have such a funny values hierarchy: a lawyer afraid of a waitress.

I ran home through the old-fashioned kiddie park, dark now. The roller coaster made the shape of a sleeping brontosaurus against the twilight sky.

"Hi, it's me. I'm here waiting for you." I never answer my phone on weekend nights as a matter of course, but I checked the message immediately. It was Rob Lowe Voice.

It was the following night and I was already in bed reading. I had taken a cucumber-melon bubble bath and painted my toenails a deep brownish red and I was just beginning to reread *The Beautiful and Damned* for about the twentieth time. Our plans had been cocktail-induced and I hadn't heard from him all day and all evening. I was exhausted and I figured since the odds are that a Seattle male will not follow through on a dating plan made at a party, it was safe for me to go to bed. It wasn't, though. He must have learned some sort of strange dating follow-through ritual in the South where he grew up.

I got up, got dressed, threw on some makeup and a toe ring, and ran down the street to the wine bar.

I saw him coming out of the bathroom and for the first time I noticed he had a slight limp and a lame hand. He had been able to compensate for his hand by holding a beer bottle with it at the party the other night. He joined me on a couch against the wall.

He ordered us a nice bottle of French white wine.

"Do you have anything pierced besides your ears? Any tattoos I should know about?" he asked.

"No . . ." I was confused, as I'm so not the pierced and tattooed type.

"I just thought with the toe ring, you know . . . it's kind of wild, isn't it? Can I see it?"

I slipped off my purple-jellybean-colored plastic flip-flops and put my feet in his lap. "Sexy," he said, reading the toe ring's stamped lettering.

After we finished the bottle of wine he walked me the two blocks home. He pointed out a big silver truck and said it was his. We passed a small house on the corner with a beautiful garden that spilled out onto the street, a midnight-purple cascade of tiny blooms, and a flat stone with engraving that read "Of all the things I've lost, I think I miss my mind the most."

Rob Lowe Voice was so young but somehow older than most of the men I date. Was it maturity born out of his intelligence? His sensitivity? His gimpiness? I did not know, but I definitely wanted to see him again. I thought.

"You should write about this," he said at my door. "The awkwardness of not knowing whether or not you should go for a kiss at the end of an evening."

I kissed him when I was already halfway inside the lobby of my building, with one hand on him and one hand holding the glass door between us. "You won't even let go of the door," he said, and smiled.

I felt terrible pangs of guilt about keeping the Web site a secret from him as I crawled into bed for the second time that night. I was not sold on him, but then I wasn't sold on anyone. At that point I was pretty sure that the phrase "It's not you, it's me" was actually true when it came to my love life.

DATE 28 The Sophomore Date Slump

TRUE CONFESSION

A beautiful black luxury car, salad made with fried bivalves, plans to go murder doves . . . it all seemed so perfect, I was quite surprised to get dumped.

"A different car each time, I like to see that," I said when Rob Lowe Voice picked me up for our second date in a slick black BMW. My last car was a fifteen-year-old Honda Accord, so the navigation system on his looked like I imagined a plane's would.

"How's your week been?" he asked.

"I had that job interview today. It was really a non-interview, as I suspect they are holding the job for a current employee but have to interview outsiders for some legal crap. It was a job *unter*-view," I said.

The company is in a gorgeous brick building that used to be a hospital. I had applied for a copyediting job and was invited there to take an editorial test, but that's it. A woman came and got me and put me in a little glass meeting room with a jaw-dropping view of Puget Sound. The test was tough, but all stuff I knew from my last job. I finished early and the woman escorted me out.

"She told me that when they called me in for a job interview, she hoped they hadn't implied that there was an actual job," I said.

"They shouldn't have told you that, legally," he said. "Do you want me to make a call?" He winked.

"I think since it was obviously a fake job interview they should have given me lunch instead of making me take a really hard test. Like: 'Thanks for showing up. We don't have an actual job for you, but here's half a turkey sub and some potato salad.'"

Rob Lowe Voice had made reservations at a Belltown seafood restaurant that epitomized Seattle before the dot-com bust. Business was booming. Waiters swept by with trays of teeny desserts drizzled in chocolate; twenty-something girls balanced their pink vodka martinis.

We were seated upstairs where it's all just tables for two. I felt great. We were one of these couples, all cozy on the balcony away from the clattering mass of singles down below. Rob Lowe Voice picked a great bottle of white wine while I put serious thought into my order. Lots of exotic sides came with the different fish, so I wanted to choose wisely. I settled on escolar with mashed potatoes, shallot jus, and picholine olive relish. I shouldn't have worried about the sides because there was about a tablespoon of each.

We started with a fried oyster Caesar salad. I had never had anything like it before and when I think of Rob Lowe Voice, it's that crunchy, creamy taste that I remember.

Though I've only met Sons o' Dixie who've emigrated to the North, my chardonnay-fueled love of Southern men was bordering on fetishist.

". . . I've met Bill Clinton and he was great," he said. "Other people from my law school class were clinging to the walls, but I met everyone at that party. Some guys don't know how to work a room . . ."

Of course they don't, but he did. He was wonderful, Bill Clinton was wonderful, I was having a wonderful time.

"It seems like we're on the same page politically," he said.

"Memphis seems so exotic to me," I purred, lulled by the good wine. He made me a little pancake from his plate with rockfish and bean sprouts, basil, mint, and coriander. I scooped some apricot anchovy salsa on it and sunk my teeth into it.

"Yeah, there are cool things that are uniquely southern. For instance I'm thinking of going dove hunting with my father and brothers next week," he said.

"People shoot those sweet little symbols of love?" I said.

"I know. I'm not much of a hunter either," he said.

It was one of those evenings when the waitress has to come back three times to get your order because you're having so much fun you forget to look at the menu. We gabbed through a bottle of wine and two rotations of other diners, then sat at our table and talked for an hour after he paid the check. The waitress may not want to see us again, but I had no doubt about us wanting to see each other.

He pulled up to the fifteen-minute parking zone in front of my building and shut off the car's engine. I looked at my hands and said, "Well."

I kissed him a few times. He looked like he wanted to say something, but didn't.

"Have fun hunting doves," I said.

"I'm not sure if I'm going hunting," he said.

I never heard from him again.

The universe sometimes presents one with an "aha" moment, presumably what happened with Ben Franklin, Thomas Edison, and Anna Nicole Smith when she married that really old rich guy. The universe can also present one with a "neener" moment. I had one such moment the very next morning. I was sitting in an overstuffed chair at Starbucks, writing in my journal about how great last night's date was, when I saw a familiar flash out of the corner of my eye. I looked up and saw that it was Rob Lowe Voice. He was reaching for the glass door from the outside, obviously about to come in, and quickly changed his mind when he saw me there. To the average person, that may not seem significant, but to a perceptive, now-expert at dating like me it didn't seem like a great sign.

I had no plans that night, which was Saturday, and I certainly didn't have a date with Rob Lowe Voice, so that evening I went for a walk past some of the little shops and restaurants in the neighborhood. As I ran across the street on my way back to my apartment, I was almost clipped by a Mercedes convertible. A middle-aged man was driving and Rob Lowe was his passenger. Not even a wave, although at least they did not hit me.

When he ignored me for the third time in twenty-four hours coming out of Blockbuster the next morning, I pretended not to see him, too.

I think the relationship gods were punishing me for thinking that I was "seeing" someone when it had only been two dates and two weeks. Sure he's too young for me, and, yes, he is looking for a job out of town, but couples have overcome worse. See, I did it again. I said *couple*. Now I definitely won't hear from him.

It has me all confused, since if I can make it past the first date, I'm usually golden. Second date and beyond, it's me who does the dumping.

I flipped through my relationship books to see where things could have gone so hideously wrong. I picked up the strictest one I could find, finding-a-husband advice from two very divorced women. I was determined not to make any more mistakes. Later that week I went to a big party a friend of mine was having and put my new, rigid ideas into practice:

CHAPTER 11: Be Mysterious

I came in through the back way and took a perch at the bar without even saying hello to anyone. Still stinging from the Rob

Lowe Voice experience and burned out on dating in general, I honestly didn't even feel like talking to anyone, but I wanted to conduct an experiment. If I did absolutely nothing—no mingling, no introductions, no eye contact from across the room even—how many guys would approach me?

CHAPTER 13: If He's Seeing Others, You Should Be Too

I instantly got some data when I was approached by a close talker from Romania who asked me what I thought of sex at first sight. He explained that he had had bad experiences with women getting upset that he didn't want to have sex right away, but that he was willing to change.

CHAPTER 28: Don't Get Hung Up on a Man Who Rejects You

I was in the midst of complaining about my unemployment with a guy who works in PR when I saw a profile I recognized. Rob Lowe Voice was chatting up a short woman with black hair and glasses. I was struck by how cute he was and floored by the fact that not only was he not calling me, he was avoiding me completely and I had no idea why. We never did talk. We never will again, I guess.

CHAPTER 40: Show Up Even If You Don't Feel Like It

I'm not feeling too optimistic about anything lately, but as Woody Allen once said, 80 percent of success is just showing up. I hope he's right. Not sure I should be taking relationship advice from Woody Allen, but then I'm not sure I should be taking advice from the divorced self-help ladies, either. Six of one . . .

BUNK DEBUNK

Myth: Never-married men over thirty-five are bad news. (Part III)

Bunked!

When I recklessly said that men are the choosers and women have to wait to be chosen, I didn't mean to imply that women over thirty-five who aren't married are somehow defective in some way. Let's face it, men can be complete idiots. I honestly don't know why we put up with them sometimes. Look, if he hasn't married you in a reasonable amount of time and he's over thirty-five and never been married, he's probably gay. That is unless you are reading this and are a man who is over thirty-five and never married, in which case my original thought about not yet finding that special lady to complete your life still stands.

DATE 29   The Handoff

TRUE CONFESSION

Since these two guys didn't know I was publicly treating men as interchangeable on my Web site, I was livid when they treated me that way.

We had the sunniest summer in the history of Seattle and then as if someone flipped a switch it became fall overnight. The gray, misty weather made me want to bake potatoes and put my feet in someone's lap. Wandering through burgundy leaves, picking out a pumpkin, reading erotic-yet-scary vampire books—those things aren't any fun without a boyfriend. Well, reading the erotic-yet-scary book is probably okay alone, but not the other stuff.

I was at a party at a modern club in old Pioneer Square. Each of the three bars was backlit in a different color, one glowing orange, the other cobalt blue, the third red.

"What do you think I should be for Halloween?" he asked.

At home with me and not at that excuse for a lingerie show that Halloween has become, I thought.

"I don't know," I said.

"I'm buying you that drink," he said.

Later . . .

"Tell me a secret," he said.

I write about men on the Internet without their permission?

"I don't have any. You tell me one."

"I call one of my friends every morning—I work with her—I call her and sing Beatles songs to her even though she's getting married soon. It's an unrequited crush."

I was developing a crush of my own. Tall, complex (a confessed social phobe), Patrick Swayze-esque—this party was looking up. Sometimes when you meet a new guy, everything just clicks. The conversation, the chemistry, the music, the alcohol.

We talked all night. I didn't want to meet anyone else and neither did he. At one point he even introduced me to his friend. He must have felt things were going well too; he wanted to show me off already. I was thrilled to overhear him tell Anastasia that her party was the best he had been to in ages because he had met me. I gave him my number and we made plans to have dinner at a quaint Moroccan place.

A week later it dawned on me that we might not be sharing couscous—or anything else—when the friend he had introduced me to at the party called and asked me out.

I was so stunned I said yes.

I was feeling totally dissed. It's bad enough when a guy decides not to call, but to pass on my number to a friend? I felt recycled. I could just imagine the conversation about my phone number: "Here, I'm not using this. Do you want it?"

I was going to be like a beautiful, yet by definition icy, Snow Queen and regally glide away from the guy who gave away my phone number.

Unfortunately, I'm not that queen. I e-mailed one line that said: "Are you planning on giving my phone number to all your friends or just the one?" He e-mailed right back to say he had lots of friends who would be interested in me and that he could put my number on a Web site if I'd like. I secretly thought it was funny but my official stance was that I was pissed.

I undermined myself slightly by shooting back: "No need to whore me out on the Internet, thanks. I can do that myself."

He went on to explain that since I knew his friend and "had more in common with him," he didn't see anything terribly wrong with giving him my number when he asked for it. I'm sure it was all very altruistic.

I had already told the friend I would go for drinks with him, and, really, why should he be punished for Tall Cute and Social Phobic's stupidity?

I was a little nervous to meet the Friend and I wondered if we were going to talk about the fact that the guy I was clearly interested in at the party wasn't the one I was with. Sometimes when a woman is in the picture, men are willing to sell out their own buddies. Or apparently hand off her phone number like it's a football. The case was clearly the latter and the first guy never even came up in conversation.

We had a drink at a slick Belltown bar. Belltown was once a slum, then it got expensive when all the rich dot-commers moved there; now that the bubble has burst, it's just populated by good restaurants and half-empty high-rises. My date looked cute. I had recently raised my standards and even though there were extenuating circumstances with this situation, I was pleased that I had not waffled on my minimum cuteness quotient.

The date was the usual getting-to-know-you stuff, broken up by a very attractive, drunken man and woman who loudly decided to exchange shirts and were soon half naked right there in the bar on a Sunday afternoon.

Despite the other guy's assurances to the contrary, I didn't think the Friend and I had tons in common.

Me: I've moved halfway across the country twice to cities where I had no job and no friends.

Him: I was born in Seattle.

Me: I've traveled around the world by myself with a backpack.

Him: I've been to Canada. I'm using my college major for my career.

Me: I don't remember what my college major was.

He wanted to continue the date, though, so we went across the street to the kitschy Polynesian-Japanese place I had gone to with the Comedian and had chicken (me) and beef (him) skewers. I zoned out toward the end of the evening like someone with a touch of autism, distracted by the glittery Lava lamps and mobiles hanging from the ceiling. When I tuned back in, he was talking about Thanksgiving.

". . . my friends and I meet halfway between our houses after dinner, just to have a drink and gather strength before going back to have pie with our families. It's hard being single around the holidays. Relatives always ask the same questions about why I'm not married yet. Just to break things up I come up with different answers. This year it's going to be that I'm gay."

DATE 30 | I Love Lucia

TRUE CONFESSION

I've been to bachelorette parties that had male strippers and they're like a miniature Mardi Gras. I've been to traditional strip joints near the airport where the men in the audience look like they're attending a wake. Can you see why I'd date a woman?

The Victorian house across the street from my apartment was ready for Halloween. Early one morning the shaggy blond guy who lives in one of its apartments dug grave-size holes in the front yard and placed gray Styrofoam RIP markers behind the freshly overturned earth. He hung small white ghosts and black bats from the trees. The orange twinkle lights he strung along the A-frame glowed against the wet, slate-colored shingles.

I had first met Lucy on the sidewalk outside the house a few weeks before. She was just moving in that evening. She was having her mattress delivered and the truck was nowhere to be found, so I let her use my cell phone to call the mattress company. She was a slim Spanish-looking woman with a soft voice. She seemed shy.

I looked out the window a few hours later and saw two men carrying a king-size bed up the stairs.

Would you like to come over and share some wine tonight?—Lucy (from across the street).

146

This was interesting. I rarely get notes left on my door. I was unemployed, broke, and desperate for entertainment. Of course I wanted to share some wine.

Unlike mine, her apartment had a view of the water and the Space Needle and downtown. It also had no furniture in the living room except for a sage green velvet chaise longue with ornate mahogany carving curled around it and down the legs. "This is beautiful," I said. It really was. "It's the only thing I took after my divorce," she said. "Good riddance." Next to it there was a little end table with white votive candles on it. The wood floor was polished like a mirror. Her apartment looked like an art gallery, the lighted ferries and black water its only painting.

We skipped the usual getting-to-know-you conversation. "The man I'm seeing was coming over the other night and I had a yeast infection, so I complained to my girl friend at work and she told me that Alka-Seltzer is a home remedy. I took two. An hour later nothing was happening, so I took two more. I asked her why it wasn't working and she laughed. I guess you're supposed to put them in you, not drink them."

I thought that was the end of it, but then I didn't know her yet. ". . . so for the rest of the day I was bubbling and making farting noises all around the office."

"This is really good wine," I said. "Yeah, it's the good stuff," she agreed, looking at her glass as it caught the candlelight. "My job is basically just a glorified receptionist, but I have a friend who sometimes gives me money. We don't have sex or anything—he's too old to get it up, but he likes to see me dress up in lingerie and walk around. Are you seeing anyone?"

Apparently my original assessment of her shyness was off. She looked like Penelope Cruz, but she acted like Lucille Ball. She should have been starring in a Spanish-dubbed *I Love Lucy*.

I told her about going on two dates with Rob Lowe Voice and ended with ". . . and then he never called again." Her anecdotes ended with ". . . and then I put on a saddle, but he wasn't into it" or ". . . and then after the dinner party I went to Las Vegas with his best friend." There was no way I could compete.

Something had been bothering me for a long time and at this point I knew Lucy would probably know the answer. "People are always implying that I'm a dominatrix. Do you know why that would be?"

"It's because of your body, hon," she said as she thumbed through the S&M section of a free weekly. "You probably have a bossy personality and that's just an added bonus."

"I agree that I have a . . . let's say, compelling . . . personality; I also consider myself a slacker. The two traits just don't go together. If I were an alpha male chimp, my group would most likely starve to death from disorganization. I don't like to give orders, I don't like to take orders—that's why I became a writer. All these 'Where's your whip, Amy?'–type comments seem really unwarranted."

After way too much wine, Lucy decided we should go out for a glass of wine.

"Oh, can't we stay here? I'm so comfortable," I drawled. Of course, I was curled up on the only piece of furniture. Lucy was sitting on a chair from the kitchen. "No! We have to go meet men," she said.

We went around the corner to a Mexican restaurant and bar that's known as a meat market. Since it was Sunday night it was quiet, though. We ordered two glasses of chardonnay that contained about half a bottle each and were nowhere near the quality of the wine Lucy was given for not having sex with her pervy old-man friend.

"Sallwomenere," she said, tapping the ashes from her cigarette into the salsa I hadn't finished yet.

"Lissen, my girls are ev'ything to me," she said. "Men are

busshit." We high-fived with both hands and she laced her fingers through mine and pulled my hands down.

We kissed at the bar—on the lips—but no guy even bought us drinks. In fact the only man we met was the bartender. He lit her cigarette after telling her to turn it around as she had the wrong end in her mouth.

I'm a few shades paler than even a lipstick lesbian, I guess. I'm a lip-gloss lesbian or a ChapStick lesbian. Nothing more happened between us. Of course in telling about our evening to boyfriends later I said, "She tasted like the taste of salt on your lips when you're near the ocean, like salt-water taffy. I nibbled her fleshy fold, her waxed skin was smooth against my cheek. It was easy to find it with my tongue, like it's easy to find my own with my hand, I sought it out, gingerly at first and then—concentrated and ex-cruciating—flicked against it again and again and faster and faster, while she said, 'Don't stop, oh, don't ever stop . . .' When I think of her, I always remember how she tasted of Alka-Seltzer."

BUNK DEBUNK

Myth: I should just become a lesbian, then dating would be simple.

Debunked!

Good Lord! I think we've all heard women say this, but even overlooking the physical aspect of it (which is fine if you're into it, but I don't think it can be suddenly proclaimed one day when you're fed up after a bad date with someone who has a penis), I'm not sure involvement with a woman means things instantly streamline. Men are simple. Men have myriad needs, but they're all different permutations having to do with food and sex. Women are complex. I've lived with myself my whole life and sometimes I don't even know what I'm thinking.

Maybe it's because I work in the arts, but it seems to me that in lots of the couples I know, the women are just more together than the men. They're certainly better at multitasking. They start businesses or write pilots for NBC or take on part-time modeling jobs in addition to working full-time and getting graduate degrees.

It's an effort for most of the men I know to take the porn off the walls when they have company over.

I suspect the explanation is partly in our genes. My girl friend Terry, who has a PhD in molecular genetics, explained it to me once: women are mosaic. Apparently our cellular makeup is literally more complex and eclectic, while that of the male is more rigid and simplistic.

I love the image it conjures of women as designed from pieces of amber and blue glass and mother-of-pearl inlaid to form an intricate, beautiful pattern. It's as evocative to me as the fact that the simple, phallic letter Y symbolizes the male chromosome. It makes perfect sense. After all, you only have to look to a bar at closing time to see how uncomplicated the male genetic code really is.

I came home that night bursting with the thrill of discovery. I had yet another clue to the differences between men and women, a new piece of knowledge to take us one step closer to community and understanding. I excitedly called my then-boyfriend, an unemployed musician, to share my news. He asked if he could call back in twenty minutes. *The Simpsons* was on and he couldn't concentrate on both of us at the same time.

DATE 31 A Boy Named Harry Potter

TRUE CONFESSION

I've been completely brainwashed and/or enlightened by dating books from the '90s and nature specials that the only way for mating to work is if the male pursues and the female is a receptive, yet constantly moving, target. I knew, though, that if I wanted to see this guy again I would have to make the first call. I had an epiphany and realized that a truly worthwhile relationship starts with equals meeting each other halfway and not outmoded role-playing. Wait, that can't be right.

We met at the last big party Anastasia's social club was having before Christmas. It was held at a popular Irish pub and there were several other parties going on there that night. It was confusing because we usually have the entire bar to ourselves. A pretty blonde woman who looked to be in her twenties and was not part of our group threw her arms around her boyfriend's neck and whispered some baby talk that I couldn't discern into his ear. "They're just trying to meet people, honey," he said, obviously defending my group, which is mostly made up of singles in their thirties and forties. I loathe smug, coupled-off people, especially if they have a mean streak, so I purposely knocked the plastic container of maraschino cherries off the bar and onto her cream-colored angora sweater. When she went to clean up in the bathroom, her boyfriend hit on me. I don't play that game, though, so I turned my attention to the band.

I was standing right in front of the stage like I always do, trying to see if the guitar player was missing any notes. I'm a former music critic.

"Are you with the band?" a slight, dark-haired guy with a goatee and round glasses like Harry Potter's asked.

"No, I just like music."

"Oh, you were looking at them so critically I assumed you were the guitar player's girlfriend. So are you in finance, too?"

"What? No. I'm a writer."

"Oh thank God. Everyone here's a banker. I look at a column of numbers and all I see is the design it makes on the paper. Hey, do you like motorcycles?"

He was a fellow artist—a fiddle player–apartment manager–graphic artist to be exact. He told me about his love of traveling to Mexico and his dislike of the Pacific Northwestern rain. We exchanged numbers.

We had been trading messages since before the holidays, but Christmas and New Year's had come and gone and we still hadn't gone out yet.

I caught him at home on a rare kind of day: it was snowing and business in the city had shut down completely. Seattle looked like a Christmas card. Cross-country skiers shushed down avenues that were normally busy with cars; children sledded down Queen Anne Hill. Harry Potter Glasses was at home roasting a turkey. My heart was warmed by his sweet domestic ways until his questions about Washington, DC, and my job as a financial adviser indicated that he didn't remember me. He admitted he talked to a lot of people at the party where we met.

Honesty rears its unwelcome face. At least when I don't remember someone who's calling me I have the decency to make fake general comments that could apply to anyone.

Didn't he realize that in dating, honesty and disclosure have no business appearing until both parties are so deeply entrenched sexually and otherwise that they are basically stuck with each other? Novice.

The snow hadn't even melted yet when we finally met for a drink at a pub near my house the next night.

I was uncharacteristically excited about this date. It probably wasn't a coincidence that it was a date I helped set up. I have this thing about not asking men out, which has morphed into not even calling them. It wasn't working too well for me.

I walked in and took a seat at the bar and grabbed a napkin and begged a pen off the bartender so I could write while I waited.

"Hi there. I'm already here."

Harry had gotten us a big wooden booth with a high back and was wearing a brown tweed jacket. He had a coffee with whiskey and cream and I had a chardonnay.

"So what else do you do besides writing if you can't find a job?" he said.

"Lately I've been selling used stuff on eBay, like designer shoes from Value Village."

"That's cool. I do the same thing sort of. I scrounge around and find junk at yard sales and make it into art. I throw big garage sales with beer and barbecue and everything. I don't do eBay, though. I don't even have a computer. I should probably get one, but I hate them. Like, people say the Internet connects us, but I think in a way it keeps us separate. Everyone typing away on their laptops, lost in their own little worlds."

He was so sweet and nontechnical. It would be really weird to tell him about the Web site.

He told me about his mom, growing up in Oregon, going to

UW. My experience with Oregon was going to Portland twice. I told him I loved the little train that travels along the forest on the hillside at the zoo. Moss the color of a yellow-green Crayola crayon is everywhere.

"My biggest star sighting as a kid was there, but you won't know who the person was: Bill Daily," he said.

"Major Healey from *I Dream of Jeannie*! Howard the pilot who lived next door to Bob and Emily!" I said. I guessed we were the same age.

He took my pen and napkin from me and drew pictures of what he had learned from a class on Frank Lloyd Wright. It was the best date I've had since starting the site. He did not ask me my age, grill me on why I haven't had children yet, or go through my hair looking for grays—all of which have happened to me in the past year.

The mainstream Sonics crowd came and went while two artists had their love-in. We were yakkityyakkityyak like old friends the whole time.

He drove me home. His car is old, with questionable seat belts. He mentioned that he had more than one car, so I wondered why he drove this one, but he did say he collects junk.

When he dropped me off he said to call him if I wanted to go out again, but I didn't. Since I don't. Call guys for dates I mean.

BUNK DEBUNK

Myth: The man has to pursue the woman in the beginning or else the relationship is doomed.

Debunked!

I was watching *Fatal Attraction* for about the dozenth time the other day and do you know that Michael Douglas absolutely chases Glenn Close for the first forty minutes of the film? Certainly that's not its reputation (it's a modern-day cautionary tale for men), but that's what happens. He approaches her at a party, he flirts, he introduces himself, he asks her out to dinner and drinks, he tells her anything that can happen is strictly up to her, because he's definitely interested. He gives nary a thought to Anne Archer, her pouty lips, ability to look great in tiny underwear, and nine-year history with him, plus the two children they have together.

Hmph, and Glenn Close is the bad guy in this story.

His pursuit of their affair is the sort of ideal that single women are told they should be looking for (except that he's married), but then look how it all turns out.

In my case, when I've let men do all the pursuing with no show of interest on my part, I've attracted those who are unable to read social cues, stalkers, and forty-somethings who live at home with their mothers in places where the curtains are drawn even during the day and the TV is on all the time.

DATE 32 The VD Outbreak

TRUE CONFESSION

Anyone who's stupid enough to go to the Cheesecake Factory on a Saturday night that's also Valentine's Day deserves whatever happens to them there.

I wanted to get sort of a "street buzz" on Valentine's Day. You know, to see if it had good word of mouth this year.

I saw a trail of conversation hearts—some crushed—on the sidewalk, but the metaphor was a bit too literal for me. I told myself that whichever one I picked up would be true for me. I selected a green one that said "U R Kind." So much for that experiment.

I fed my eavesdropping habit at the bus stop. A young guy with bleached-blond hair was having a warm conversation on his cell phone. "You should listen to track four on the CD I burned for you. It will get you through this, I swear. I'll be home in a minute anyway. I love you.

"That was a nice conversation to have with an ex," he said to me. "I mean what am I supposed to do?" he continued with no encouragement on my part. "We've been together for three years. That's forever in gay men's time. Am I supposed to just move my stuff out? I hate moving, so we keep just getting back together."

"And you're really young," I ventured. "Three years is probably a big chunk of your dating life."

"You're right," he said. "I should probably get back out there while I still look good."

Valentine's Day is overhyped and offends me with its commercialism. Thank God I had a date for it. It was a blind date with a guy who had won one of my eBay auctions. The auction was called I Will Ask Someone on a Date for You. A guy paid $13 to have me ask myself out on his behalf. After a few awkward phone calls and uncomfortable silences ("Did you say something?" "No, I thought you said something."), I finally got a date with myself, mostly to get myself off the phone.

Like me, he has been a music critic and aspires to write funny little memoirs. The thing that made me agree to meet him was a sweet story he had written about going on a game show. He was anxious that the other contestants like him and ended up doing things like carrying their bags through hotel lobbies for them.

Although he planned three weeks in advance, the only reservations we could get were those to wait in line for at least an hour at the Cheesecake Factory downtown. For those who aren't familiar with this chain (i.e., foreigners), it is aptly named. It has cheesecake and it is run like a factory. When you join your fellow potential diners in the lobby, you are given a beeper that will start flashing when your number is up. Or when they have a table for you, whichever comes first.

Although we had just exchanged head shots, I recognized him right away. He was wearing a bright red shirt, which I thought was cute, because if you're going to have dinner on Valentine's Day with a stranger who writes about her dates on the Internet, it would just be sad to try to play it cool.

He had a smirky, sideways-glancing quality about him as if we were both hipsters who knew something others didn't, even though, really, we weren't.

"Those girls behind us were talking about applying to some-apparently-local-school-that-meant-nothing-to-me. They're idiots," he said by way of introduction.

"Ah," I said, not at all grasping the subtext or even the actual text.

He worked at a local arts weekly. Seattle already supports two bigger weeklies; this was one of the second-tier ones and the staff was mostly made up of volunteers.

I felt like a sham. I'd never written for anything even remotely hip, only commercial entities. I scrambled for something cool I'd written for and then I remembered *BAM*, which was the California sister to Seattle's dearly departed music magazine *The Rocket*. I told him so.

"They won't let me write music reviews for the magazine anymore," he said. "I was too vicious."

Whenever two music critics get together, the conversation invariably turns to bands that no one's ever heard of except music critics, but often they're not the same bands. The conversation goes like:

"Have you heard of the Shins?"

"No, but I like the Shakes."

"I don't know them but lately I've been listening to the Vespas."

"I don't think I've heard them, but have you heard of . . ."

This can go on for up to forty-five minutes. We stopped after about ten.

It turned out he had never had a paid writing job. I lied that staff writing jobs weren't that great.

"Tell that to my last girlfriend," he said sideways. "She was always harping on me to get paid for my writing. She remembered to remind me of that as often as possible, but forgot to tell me she had a sexually transmitted disease, so go figure."

The lobby was filled with increasingly stale air and impatient people dressed in pink and red and white. After standing for forty-five minutes, the guy next to me literally collapsed into a diabetic coma—extreme even for the Cheesecake Factory, where most people just look like they're going to. The quick-thinking manager forced a piece of Baileys Original Irish Cream cheesecake into the man's mouth to increase his insulin level. When the paramedics arrived I daintily stepped over his body and continued my analysis of the impact of the Smiths. It was okay, though, I was wearing panties.

One hour and countless other couples later, we were led to our booth. The waitress appeared.

"Did you wait long?"

"If by 'long' you mean the amount of time it takes to adopt a baby from China, then no," my date said.

I had two glasses of pinot gris, lemon herb chicken with mashed potatoes and carrots. He had some spicy shrimp and pasta and a Sam Adams. We had coffee and split a piece of vanilla-bean cheesecake, which he batted me away from with his fork when I crossed over to his side of the plate.

Dinner took hours, but I was having fun.

The only weird thing was that although he offered to walk me to the bus stop, he didn't offer me a ride home. It was the first time in the course of our four-hour relationship that he had done that and it seemed totally out of character.

A few weeks later a guy from a band who said he had once been reviewed by my Valentine's date sent me a link to a Web site where the guy had written about our dinner together. Apparently the reason he had left me at a bus stop downtown at 10:00 p.m. was because he saw "the woman he was supposed to marry" standing on the sidewalk while I was in the bathroom. He needed to get rid of me so he could run back, introduce himself, and they could begin their life together. Sadly for him, by the time he got back to the restaurant, she had gone home with her boyfriend.

The way he wrote about himself wearing his bright red shirt and walking to his car after finding the other woman gone made him sound poignant like that photo of James Dean with the collar of his overcoat turned up against the sleet as he walked down Hollywood Boulevard.

It's funny how we always cast ourselves as the romantic heroes of our own stories.

In my version he was just an asshole.

BUNK DEBUNK

Myth: A man will tell you who he is within the first five minutes.

Bunked!

I've actually had guys say, "I'm a flake," or "I'm an asshole." And they should know, right?

I met a man for dinner once and the first thing he said was something cruel about the hostess. He then went on to criticize his mother. Dudeman, we just met. Don't be dissing your mommy to me!

Ladies, if you pay attention, your first conversation with a man is the crystal ball that will show you your future with him.

Unless he's a sociopath, in which case never mind.

DATE 33 Looking for Elvis

TRUE CONFESSION

I'm perhaps guiltier than most of searching for an ideal when it comes to romance. After I met Paul Westerberg from the Replacements, not only a hero from my hometown of Minneapolis but an alternative rock icon, I didn't look at any regular guy for two months. Sometimes I'm searching only for stardust rather than an actual star, though.

One of the thrift stores I go to for the secondhand designer shoes I sell on eBay was doing a '50s theme for a month. Every time a customer spent $50, they got a Sockhop to Savings card which was good for a 30 percent discount on their next purchase. The card would then be entered into a drawing for a $6,000 CD-playing jukebox that lights up in neon. We used to have one in the lobby of a dot-com I worked for until some men in gray jumpsuits came and wheeled it away when we couldn't pay the electric bill that quarter. They're beautiful.

To add to the malt shop ambience, the thrift store was playing an endless loop of music you'd find in a real '50s jukebox. It's depressing for me to hear chirpy Eisenhower-era optimism while I embody the Bush Jr. era: unemployed, the smell of stale used clothing seeping through the surgical mask I wear to keep out the dust and mold as I pick through other people's discarded shoes.

Then the tape got to "Hound Dog."

The dingy store brightened a bit. I stood a little straighter. Maybe I would get a book deal. And, hey, at least I was making money with eBay. It could be worse. It could be a lot worse.

While I have nothing against the Shirelles or Ricky Nelson, every time Elvis comes on he seems as bright and misplaced against his contemporaries as the neon CD jukebox does compared to those little jukeboxes you see in booths at rural diners. He just sounds so . . . charged.

That night I had a déjà rock. Anastasia was having a party at the Hendrix museum. I thought the party would be dull, but she is good at promotions, so I stopped by—just for an hour—to talk to her about whether or not I should get advertisers for my Web site. Three hours and two glasses of merlot later I was being chatted up by several swing-dancers while a local radio station was broadcasting its '50s music show *Shake the Shack* a few feet away from us. I was gracefully declining my second offer to join the few half-hearted dancers in front of the DJ table when Elvis's "Little Sister" came on. "Do you want to dance?" I shouted to the man next to me. A crowd suddenly descended onto the tiny space, so I know it wasn't just me.

As the party was winding down, a guy I was talking to was itemizing the nine singles clubs to which he belongs. He has a lifetime membership to four of them. I realized I'd met him at a party in December when he was talking about the exact same thing.

Not only were the men I was meeting repeating themselves, the patterns of the men I was meeting were repeating themselves. Show some skin and the gorgeous, much younger guys with lots of money come around. Mention writing and guys dressed in black want to talk about art over sushi.

It occurred to me that my downfall had been to look for someone who didn't fit the pattern, the Elvis song on a '50s jukebox, a relationship that was . . . charged. But that hadn't happened to me in years. Maybe as you get older it can't happen like that anymore? I told myself that I could probably be just as happy with Buddy Holly.

The people at the party were nice enough, but they had a mainstream feel that was somehow like polyester. Not the hip, musty polyester of the thrift store, but the new kind. There was one man who stood out. He had longish, very curly dark hair and was wearing a sports jacket over a Social Distortion T-shirt. He was a music critic for a local newspaper and I couldn't help but think of how a disproportionate number of gynecologists are named Hymen when he introduced himself as Eric Van Halen.

"I've never met anyone named Van Halen," I said. "You don't look very Dutch, though." It was a few nights later and we were having drinks at a Mexican bar in my neighborhood.

"I'm Puerto Rican on my mother's side."

"Are you any relation?"

"No, but my dad was in a band when I was growing up. When I was little I thought our Van Halen albums were his band."

It seems like every male music critic I know has a dad who was a musician. Oedipal resolution by arts journalism, apparently.

We were perched on high stools at a counter next to windows facing the street. I was wearing a mid-thigh-length skirt that kept hiking up. I felt awkward. I didn't feel like talking to anyone and I wasn't really in a dating kind of place. The last man I'd gone out with had deserted me at a bus stop at 10:00 p.m. because he thought he'd glimpsed the woman he was meant to be with outside a restaurant downtown.

Eric was so sweet that those feelings faded as quickly as the Clairol Natural Instincts in Rio Red Ginger that I sometimes use on my hair.

I was wearing a leather jacket I hadn't worn since the party where I met him when I remembered too late that the zipper was broken. I had lost part of the zipper at the party, and in a typically drunken scenario, many people were helping me look for the tiny thing on the floor of the dark bar as if it were a contact lens. We never found it. Now I was all zipped up and feeling a tightness across my bust, since the jacket is a 38 and I'm a 39 at least.

"I can't unzip my jacket!" I said to Eric, in what was starting to be a panic.

"No, there's still a little metal tag left here," he said, and unzipped it for me.

I realized that's what'd been missing from most of my other dates: a sense of intimacy.

I had my usual chardonnay and we shared Mexican spring rolls, a surprising combination that came with two dipping sauces—hot salsa and plum.

He brought his laptop to the bar so I could read the novel he was writing, but I declined on the grounds that I couldn't see well enough. I could have read by the flickering candlelight, I guess, but it seemed silly to read it at a bar. I understood the sentiment, even though I couldn't relate to it. The Web site was getting thousands of visits a day. I was getting more attention for my writing than any unpublished writer I knew.

"My novel's like *The Man Show*," he said, referring to something I was pretty sure opened with braless women bouncing on a trampoline and was also off the air. "My life is kind of like *The Man Show*, now that I think of it, I live with a bunch of guys in a big house. We talk about things like hockey."

I was impressed that he had moved to Seattle during the worst part of our economic depression here and within a month got a writing job he loves. I liked him. I thought he liked me too.

"Let's do this again. You're awesome," he said, zipping up my jacket as we were getting ready to leave.

Our cocktail waitress looked like Britney Spears. She caught me as I was on my way out of the ladies' room to tell me that my date had left. Apparently he thought he saw his soul mate drive by and wanted to catch her.

Kidding.

DATE 34 Harry Potter and the One My Readers Talked Me Into

TRUE CONFESSION

My own judgment about which men to date is so severely impaired that I actually let my readers—total strangers—shame me into calling Harry Potter after our first date because I said how much I liked him on my Web site.

Some of the guys who read my Web site really had their man-skirts in a bunch over the fact that I didn't call the artist with the Harry Potter glasses that I had had a good time with at the Irish bar. Apparently they were clinging to the shred of interest he showed when he'd said, "Call me." Those guys would not last as women for five minutes because anything in reference to calling at the end of a date (especially "I'll call ya") has to be tuned out faster than a smooth-jazz station.

As pleased as I was to see my readers using words like *antiquated* correctly, could they really believe that I was wrong not to call a man after a date?

Obviously they needed a little science refresher. There are two chemical compounds that make men chase women: testosterone and alcohol. If men don't have enough of one, they can always rely on the other. Women have only one of those options, and even then we just look sloppy and pathetic. In any event, I don't think men are that meek when they're interested. I've seen a clinically diagnosed social phobe call a woman to ask her out. It took him all day, but still.

Was there really anyone out there who thought that this guy was sitting at home desperately wanting to ask me out, but not doing so because I didn't call him? That he was fretting, "Why, why did she not call? Why?" Not unless he's secretly female. Sorry, but until he's really involved, even the nicest guy usually views women as interchangeable.

"I dig Asian girls." "I like redheads." "I only date blonde model types." Have you ever heard a woman utter this kind of crap?

For example, I once again ran my eBay auction I Will Ask Someone on a Date for You. I let people bid on the chance to have me call someone they were too shy to call and ask them on a date. I knew it would be so sweet and poignant, something to renew my jaded spirit.

A college student from the University of Colorado won and for $14 had me invite a girl in his chemistry study group to the Olive Garden. She was so flattered when I called. The next week I followed up with him to see what had happened on the dream date I had set up.

"She had her friend call me and cancel for her at the last minute," he said.

Oh God, how awful! I thought. He's been pining for her and was willing to pay someone from the Internet to ask her out. I knew he must be crushed.

"It was no big deal," he said. "I just went out with the friend who called instead."

Men are resilient and so I couldn't believe that Harry Potter was dying to see me again and just too scared to pick up the phone. Then again, we had had a great time on our first date, so I took my readers' advice and called him. He asked me out immediately.

Honestly, though, as effortless as it felt to be with him, getting him to pursue me reminded me of trying to start my car when it was parked outside my apartment building in December in Minnesota. Sitting there with the key in the ignition saying, "Come on, come on, turn over." Once it caught it was fine, but getting it to start first thing in the morning was a hassle.

Harry and I agreed to meet at a coffee shop near my house, even though I don't do coffee-only dates at night usually. He was on time and starving, so we went to dinner. You can always tell Seattle natives by the restaurants and bars they choose; they will pick a place that's William H. Macy rather than Freddie Prinze Jr.

He took me to a Mexican place he used to go to in college. A hole-in-the-wall with food awards on its goldenrod walls. We ordered goblets of potent margaritas over ice with chunky salt on the rims. A pudgy waiter with stubby fingers brought us green and red salsa with thick corn chips. Harry had chicken mole and I had a chicken quesadilla that seemed to be made with Velveeta.

"I really needed this food," he said. "My friends sometimes stop by and hang out at my studio while I work and today we were drinking beer all afternoon."

"Your friends don't work?"

"Well, we were keeping one of the guys who lives in my building company. He's a heroin addict and he's trying to quit, but it's like he needs something and beer is better than heroin, so . . ."

"Wow. I've never known a heroin addict. That I know of."

"He drives me nuts. He's like this hippie, dippy San Francisco guy. Everything is about peace and positive vibes. He grew up in Haight Ashbury—he really didn't stand a chance of not being a junkie. We try to scare him straight by telling him his girlfriend is going to leave him if he doesn't get off drugs and get a job. She's really cute."

Jeez. Even heroin addicts have someone and I don't. I guess I shouldn't be surprised, lots of them have more successful careers in the arts than I do, too.

"Then my other friend who's a cross-dresser came over. He's a painter too."

"Sounds like quite a crew. I love men in dresses."

"Lots of women do."

"Is he straight?"

"Very. I swear sometimes I think he plays up the skirts and accessories just to attract women. My friends aren't all that out there, though," he said. "One of my other friends is an airline mechanic. He wouldn't sign off on that plane that ended up crashing a few years ago. It wasn't passing inspection and the Powers That Be said to sign off on it anyway."

"Oh God, I'm terrified to fly," I said. "You mean they actually knew there was something wrong with it before it took off?"

"Yeah, I guess they lose money if they don't keep to their schedule, so safety isn't their first consideration."

"And your friend got fired?"

"No, but he couldn't stand to work there anymore. Some people did get fired, but of course it was none of the higher-ups; it's always some poor low-level mechanic who probably didn't want to okay the plane anyway. People in power might pay on some level, but they never really pay in the way they should, you know?"

"Like making them fly on a plane they themselves said was 'fine' or something?"

"Yeah."

We agreed about big things—values, politics, how the world should work. And bigger things—that Day of the Dead in Oaxaca would be the perfect vacation, that at the end of *Run Lola Run*, when her boyfriend says, "So what's in the bag?" it's just perfect. He even loves Django Reinhardt.

"Where to next?" he asked.

"I don't care. Whatever you want to do."

"Nope. I asked you first." Everything is fifty/fifty with him, which surprisingly bothers me. We went back to the coffee place, and if I didn't know better I could swear he purposely ducked into the bathroom when our coffee was ready so I'd have to pay for it.

An Italian toddler wandered over to our table. I don't think he was old enough to speak. It reminded me of being in Italy—little kids out with their families at 10:30 at night.

"She's amazing, isn't she?" Harry said as the child stared at me. The child didn't answer.

"Wow, we do have a really great time together," Harry said as he was dropping me off. It was as if he were weighing things in his mind. There was a really big "but . . ." hanging out there. Its crack was showing. It either needed to lose a few pounds or get some pants that fit. I suspected the "but . . ." was another woman he was already involved with.

I told myself that if things didn't get off the ground with him, I was going on a romance hiatus for a while. Dating was becoming a grind. And not the good kind.

At least he didn't say "Call me" again.

BUNK DEBUNK

Myth: *Don't worry, someone better will come along.*

Debunked!

It would be more accurate for people to say that there's someone better *out there*. This is true since it's not like they're saying you're going to meet this better person or that the better one is available or that they'd want you if they were (which, let's face it, "someone better" probably isn't going to be single for long, so even in the best-case scenario your window of opportunity isn't going to be huge and what if they live in Bangladesh or Cleveland?). At some point, you really will have dated the best person you're ever going to get.

DATE 35 Hiking in Heels

TRUE CONFESSION

Deep down I want a man to drop me off at the restaurant if he has to park half a mile away or it's raining or I'm in heels. I know it's not fair, but then neither is the income gap or the fact that he's wearing loafers.

One of the best things about a second date is that I already know I kinda like the guy which means I am willing to ride in his car which means I can wear impractical shoes. The strappy slingbacks were Italian patent leather, my date was Eric Van Halen.

We had plans to go to the Seattle Art Museum, but since it was Friday night, it was closed. He suggested that we walk around Pike Market, which, since it was Friday night, was also closed.

I'm a patient gal. I read that book by the three New York guys about what men want. They say that when a man's date plans fall through, he is lost. I was sweet and waited for Eric to come up with another plan. His plan was that we browse around a political bookstore. The store is okay—someplace I would support more in theory than with Visa, but at least it made fun of Republicans a lot. As I was halfheartedly picking up political books and putting them down, Eric started stroking my back and trying to be romantic. One thing that always astonishes me about men is their gumption. His plan fell through and so he was putting the moves on me while I politely pretended to be interested in browsing at a bookstore? The cartoon bubble over my head said "Not without dinner first" while he mentally fumbled for the switch to the lightbulb over his.

After a thousand eternities in which the universe collapsed upon itself and then was reborn from the first amoeba sprouting legs and crawling triumphantly out of the muck to the nuclear holocaust that our current administration seems bent upon, Eric suggested dinner at a nearby brewpub.

It was one of those commercial places that makes up for its lack of imagination by being overly air-conditioned. I hate those places. At the table next to us a sorority was having a birthday party for one of the girls. Their balloons and cosmopolitans were the color of dark pink carnations.

Eric was a gentleman. He even pulled out my very high stool for me, something I don't think I've had a guy who wasn't a maître d' do since the high school prom. Eric was also not a gentleman. I had gotten used to his habit of talking to my breasts, but for some reason I was caught by surprise when he ordered two pints of beer from the cocktail waitress's nipples.

There are several restaurant games that people play when they are (1) treating, (2) don't want to spend much, and (3) don't want you to either. These include, but are not limited to, saying, "Oh, the appetizers sound good!" or "I just feel like something light," which are in reality strongly worded suggestions and not passing comments. Eric chose an old favorite:

Him: I was thinking of ordering the chicken wings.

Me: Sounds great, I think I'll have the chicken quesadilla.

Him: Yes, that does sound better.

Him (*to the nipples*): We'll have the quesadilla, and could you bring two plates?

Our dinner conversation was an exact replica of the conversation we had on our first date, which made me wonder how many women he's seeing. I couldn't bear to think it was just that he had no imagination. For my part I kept saying, "Oh, that store had *The Devil in the White City*, that book you recommended . . ." about a book he didn't recommend and "I loved how you described the Yeah, Yeah, Yeahs," when he had never heard of them. We are both clearly victims of TMD—too much dating.

He wanted to go to a club with live music called the Tractor Tavern. It's in a different part of town that used to be blue-collar and Scandinavian and is now expensive and hip. He parked and we had to hike there—me in my Italian-and-only-for-riding-around-in-a-car heels. When we got to the door, I felt him flinch at the $20 cover, so I graciously declared that I didn't care for that band anyway. I suggested coffee, but was then punished by the gods because we had to hike about a mile to the nearest coffee place—and it was not even a cool, independent coffeehouse, but was rather a Tully's. My feet were screaming at me to start dating men who are better planners.

When we mercifully arrived for coffee, I ordered a latte and offered to pay for a cream cheese brownie, which was actually a test of my own and not a real offer. He accepted and concurrently failed. He had never had one, which made me sorry for him. We sat at what was literally a children's table with blocks and stuffed furniture next to us and I cut the brownie in half and served him his portion. It was accidentally and suddenly maternal and the brownie was too rich for me, although Eric clearly wasn't.

As my poor feet and I began our long walk back to the truck with Eric, he asked if I had ever been married.

"Nope." I was cranky by this time.

"I used to be married," he said. "I liked it. Would you like to get married?"

"Not right now."

"I don't have to get married again," he said. "Living together would be fine."

I find that if I'm losing interest in a guy I become more easy-going than if I am serious about him. There's no need to hold fast to strident rules like who pays for what or where things are going if I know we're not going to end up together anyway. This low-pressure approach of course makes me more appealing to the men I don't see as real contenders and less appealing to the ones I do, who are expected to adhere to rigid guidelines which may or may not be stated.

People who date a lot lead irony-filled lives.

DATE 36 Harry Potter and the Pink Corridor

TRUE CONFESSION

There seems to be an inverse relationship between how interesting a man is and how much he has to spend to make a date fun.

The beautiful blond couple faced each other in the lemony morning sun. Naked, innocent, and perfect. They were without shame, they were without genitalia.

Harry Potter and I had wandered into a yard sale and he had found a box of nude Barbie dolls.

"It's a plastic orgy," he said. He plucked out a Ken with a vapid expression and impossibly blue eyes and a Barbie with tiny *B* for Barbie logos where her panties should have been.

"I'm Aryan Nation Ken," Harry said. "Barbie needs hydrocortisone for that B-shaped rash on her butt."

I was excited about this date, because my current favorite guy, Harry Potter Glasses, was taking me to my current favorite brunch place. It has a white picket fence and the omelets come with a side of homemade coffee cake. They have a pot of coffee outside for the people waiting to get in, so we grabbed two cups of it and went to explore some nearby buildings.

Harry has a degree in art and is constantly pointing out design elements that most people take for granted—mint green trim against a brick-colored house or the shine of a brewery's cement floor. "I like that patina. It's really beautiful," he said as we walked back to the restaurant.

As soon as we sat down to eat I felt uncomfortable. As we had our garden omelets with hash browns and coffee cake on the side, tousled couples in sweats who obviously had just gotten out of bed together were nuzzling each other all around us. There's an intimacy to spending Sunday morning with someone and I didn't really know Harry yet at all. I was looking forward to one thing: we were going to see the cherry trees blooming at the arboretum. They were the stuff of Washington mythology.

After brunch we got in the car to leave and Harry punctuated his opinion of the aspirations of the middle class by accelerating over the cement parking divider and right through the restaurant's white picket fence. He got out to assess the damage and went back inside without a word. A few minutes later I really was in Harry Potter's car as three waiters and a cook lifted it into the air and Harry jumped in at the last minute to steer. We drove to the arboretum.

I wanted to see the Japanese garden since I assumed the cherry trees would be there. They weren't, but lots of huge, ugly koi fish were. Harry hung back and let me pay our entry fee. We walked through the very small garden which was the spiritual equivalent of a miniature golf course. Harry admired the patina of a mock-Japanese roof.

"I'm big on patina today," he said. "God, your hair is really auburn in the sunshine."

We left the garden and walked for miles. We strolled through a meadow past a greenhouse. He told me that when he was a kid and he and his family went on vacations his dad would film his brother and him alternately getting out of the car to point at objects of interest.

"He tried to save tape by filming things in slow motion, so when we would watch home movies it would look like my brother and I were in a hyperactive frenzy to stand near giant sequoias and point at plaques on buildings."

A wooden dock took us through a marsh that had ducks and geese and boaters. A boat motored past and Harry sounded excited when he said, "Bush has a boat like that!"

This was interesting. Enthusiasm about anything having to do with Bush? Was Harry a closet Republican? Perhaps he was more complex than the ultraliberal I was characterizing him as, but then . . .

"So, do you like him?" I asked. Lawyers call this leading.

"Oh God no. I can't even look at him. He makes me sick."

Stereotype intact, we walked back to his old car. As we were rattling home we found our second yard sale and plastic blond couple of the day. She was putting out last season's Ferragamo shoes and he was on his cell phone talking about briefs—legal not Hanes.

"I don't know how people in their thirties can even afford a house here."

That was more disturbing to me than the Barbie doll's B-shaped rash. I understand not having money, but not even being able to imagine it? The people who lived in those houses probably had jobs. When my parents were in their thirties they had a far bigger house and yard than the blond couple.

I'm a socialist, but it's mostly circumstantial. I deeply believe that the wealthy should pitch in to support the less financially privileged, and that the distribution of assets should be overseen by someone, because left to their own devices people tend to want to keep the money they've earned and spend it on themselves or their loved ones rather than giving it away to strangers like me.

That's how I feel when I'm not working. When I am earning a

lot of money I'm a staunch capitalist, so I can see the value of both theories.

Harry is a dedicated lefty, which I enjoy, and a forty-four-year-old angry young man, which I can tolerate, except it seemed to be directed at everyone that day.

The patina was definitely coming off the rose. And I still had yet to see any cherry trees.

Although it could have been part of their plot to anesthetize the left wing, the hateful blond capitalist home owners having the yard sale took time out from disregarding the poor by giving Harry several dozen cans of paint for his interior design work and helping him load it into the back of his car.

As we pulled out of the alley of the pretty neighborhood, Harry had to back up to let a woman out of her driveway. "People are so inconsiderate," he said, unfairly I thought, since it was a narrow alley and she did have a constitutional right to leave her house.

We started home. I was cranky now, too. As if to mirror the mood inside the car, the late-afternoon traffic squeaked to a warm, dusty halt. I looked to my right and when we began moving again I asked Harry to pull over.

There were the cherry trees. A lush corridor of frosty pink milk-shakes in the afternoon heat.

They were beautiful.

BUNK DEBUNK

Myth: Women want rich guys because of their money.

Debunked!

Women do love wealthy men, but it's not because of their money. It's because of the qualities the men have that helped them *get* the money. For example, Bill Gates has *smarts*, Donald Trump has *negotiating skills*, mobster kingpins have lots of *friends*.

A guy with family money and not much else couldn't get a date with a single mom desperate for a night out even if he offered to pay for the baby-sitter. Not sure where someone with family money like John F. Kennedy Jr. fits in except that he looked like John F. Kennedy Jr.

DATE 38/37   Two Dates in Reverse

DATE 38

3:00 a.m. on Friday

I'm in the backseat of a silver rental car parked three blocks from my house. I wake up with a start and my arm hurts since it's pressed into the seat belt. I'm wearing black low-rise pants that are hot since they're a wool blend, a black tank top from the Gap, and a 200-pound guy. Teflon's hair is short and spiky and so soft. My fingers are dug into it. I nudge him with my elbow since it's the only thing that's free.

"At least I should go home," I say.

"I have to be at work in a few hours anyway. Just go back to sleep," he says as a black Mercedes pulls into the apartment building we're parked in front of.

My mind briefly flashes on something I heard recently about what men think of women who get into the backseats of cars with them and then I drift off.

11:00 p.m. on Thursday

I don't want to invite him in because it's technically only our second date and I pretty much know we're both seeing other people. We like to kiss a lot and the only solution I can see is the backseat. He goes outside and I shimmy through the space between the front seats and as we fall into each other's arms a couple driving by in an SUV give us a thumbs-up. They can see us since the overhead light is still on.

9:51 p.m. on Thursday

"Do you mind if we stop into my office for a minute? I want to shut off my computer."

His company is like a hip dot-com, but solvent. He has a view of some gorgeous old buildings in Pioneer Square.

"Keep in mind that the car I have is a rental. It's not sexy like the one I own."

We're in the elevator and as the doors shut he kisses me and puts his hand down the back of my pants and lightly squeezes the top of my cheek. We respectably break apart a second before the doors open, although there's no one to see us anyway.

9:30 p.m. on Thursday

"Do you want me to walk you home or do you want to go get my car at work and I can drive you back?"

"Which do you think is closer?"

"They're equidistant. It's up to you, sweetie."

"I'm a little cold."

He hails a cab. We are completely, politely silent in deference to the driver. Teflon has his hand on my thigh the whole ride.

"Have you been in the Elvis cab?" I lean over and whisper.

"No."

"Have you heard of it?"

"Yes."

The Elvis cab is, as its name implies, a cab driven by an Elvis impersonator. It's been written up in the paper.

9:00 p.m. on Thursday

We're at a hip Belltown bar. Girls with lace skirts and magenta hair walk by and my wine is fantastic. He's having a Hefeweizen with a slice of lemon floating in it. There's a lamp made out of a boar's leg in the corner and the leather couch is so soft I put my nose to it and inhale. I'm wearing three fragile glass bracelets, burgundy with gold glitter. I gesture and put my arm on the wooden back of the couch and one of the bracelets shatters. Then another. Now I'm wearing just one. "Come on, no one's around us," he says, and kisses me again.

7:12 p.m. on Thursday

Him: If you don't feel well we can just call it a night. I guess . . .

I like him and the night is really going to end before it starts if I don't think fast.

Me: No. I'm just weird tonight, really. Let's go have fun. Let's get a drink.

7:00 p.m. on Thursday

I'm in the restaurant bathroom washing my hands. There is a TV in the wall above the sink showing a cautionary sex ed video from the '50s. The message is that girls think they'll be more popular with boys if they get in the backseat of cars, but that those girls don't get asked out on nice dates.

6:15 p.m. on Thursday

Dinner is amazing. The restaurant is a converted theater with pink blown glass caught in fishing nets hanging from the ceiling. I'm having halibut wrapped in paper-thin potatoes. He is having sashimi. We're both having a stilted conversation. I'm jittery and the conversation has the feel of dishes rattling on a metal pushcart. He actually asks me if I'm okay.

6:00 p.m. on Thursday

Fuck. I'm already late as I get on the bus and then of course in the free-ride area it has to stop to pick up the drunks and wheelchair-bound homeless who will only ride two blocks anyway. I'm on the way to meet Teflon for dinner. I do like him and we are a bit beyond small talk. When I was in grade school we were taught to remember the rainbow with the acronym ROY G. BIV. I'm in the green, middle area of the color spectrum where I'm not red, close enough to spill everything about the site, but then again I want him to know me a little more than in the violet sense. My nerves are coiled and the guy wearing a name tag that says Hello, My Name Is Michael Stipe is taking forever to get his shopping cart off the bus.

DATE 37

9:30 p.m. on Monday

"The key goes in the lock like this," some black-haired punk-ass kid who lives in my building says sarcastically as he and his girlfriend open the door and walk down the hall to get their laundry. My date and I linger in the alley between my building and the one next door. There are magenta and white flowers tumbling over the railings and a coffee can with sand and cigarette butts stuck in it on the other building's steps.

"Before I forget . . ." he says, and pulls the book *Running with Scissors* out of his backpack. He gives it to me. I go to hug him and we kiss for the first time. It feels great.

9:00 p.m. on Monday

He offers to walk me home, which is sweet because it's at least a mile, although it's a total deal breaker if not offered, something that has happened to me more than once. We walk down the main drag and those restaurants that are open are brimming with people drinking, laughing, eating at sidewalk tables. He holds my hand, which always feels premature and serious to me on a first date. When I drop it he comments that that's one way a guy tells whether or not someone is into him. He reminds me that when we met he had his arm around me and that later I asked if he would put it around me again. I cringe and deny this revelation and then vaguely remember it. He tells me I'm like a tough girl who really isn't tough at all.

8:00 p.m. on Monday

We're at another place with an almost-view of the water and a very real view of the tourists tromping down the alley with their strollers and their balloons. We're in Pike Market on the narrow patio of an Irish pub. I don't remember what we talked about, but I do remember thinking that I liked him and that things were going well.

7:35 p.m. on Monday

Me: Shall we go?

7:15 p.m. on Monday

Seattle doesn't have much of a view when you are on land and looking at the water. Not like my last residence, Santa Monica, where you can be standing in Palisades Park and look to the left and see the Santa Monica Pier with the carousel above which Paul Newman lived in *The Sting* and look to the right and see the necklace of early evening lights that are Malibu and then look straight ahead to see the sun drifting down between the fog and the palm trees and the dark pink bougainvillea.

The view from the pier in Seattle is water, the occasional ferry, and the promise of islands near Canada. Teflon and I rightly turn our attention to the land.

"It's the longest day of the year," he says as the sun beats down on us.

"I can't believe Seattle was fourth in line for an attack on 9/11.

They must have been considering that building," I say, indicating the big, black Bank of America tower.

"When are they going to raise the flags from half mast?" he says. Ronald Reagan has just died.

I'm going to give him approximately twenty more minutes to get up the nerve to kiss me and then I will make an executive decision to go elsewhere, because the midsummer evening sun is relentless.

7:00 p.m. on Monday

We walk down to the waterfront. I've never been there. We pass the junkies on the stairs, the restaurant where you can get a whole lobster boiled in front of you, the storefront filled with mounted moose heads and antelope parts. There's a sprawling outdoor patio, but we bypass it to sit on a bench at the water's edge.

6:00 p.m. on Monday

I show up at the bar—relatively on time for me—and he is waiting inside. We are meeting because he is lending me a book and has offered to buy me a drink. We snare a seat outside on the tiny patio that has a quasi ocean view if you turn your head. I have chardonnay and he has beer. We talk about Europe and dating in Seattle and he orders us some pâté ("It's like ham spread for grown-ups," he says). He tells me that he got into a car accident the day before. No one was hurt but he is renting a car now. I tell him that my friend Darren once had someone back into him at a stoplight and he was still found at fault. Teflon says he has never heard of anyone hitting a car by backing up. He was on his way to a beer festival when the accident happened. His booming social life depresses me even as it is one of my requirements for anyone I'd date seriously—I don't have one since I'm a misanthrope, but I do love to hear about any good parties.

Friday, 2:11 a.m.

"I don't have my car with me, but I have to see you home. Without you dealing with all the speaking-Italian craziness."

"I'll just walk home. It's not that far. I do it all the time."

"No way, I'll put you in a cab or something," he says.

"There are no cabs in Seattle."

We look out the window and seven cabs in a row speed by.

He arranges a ride for me with one of the women. I'm sitting in her car and he crouches in the open passenger-side door. He kisses my hand and shuts the door. His lips feel good on my skin.

Friday, 1:30 a.m.

The seven of us stumble across the street for a late, late dinner. One of the busty blondes says we can get special treatment since she knows the hostess. The hostess does indeed seat us in the dinner area which is closed . . . and has menus at twice the price of the bar. We migrate back to the bar area and beg the waiter to let us order something. We have a confusing dinner of little pizzas and fried pickles with ranch sauce. It's so good. We've lost the blond volleyball player to a group of hot Asian chicks and the two blondes are refusing to speak anything but Italian. Now it really is time to go.

Thursday, 11:45 p.m.

He and his friends—an absurdly tall guy and a California volleyball type—corral me and three other busty women to go for drinks in Belltown with them.

The bar is packed, but for some reason a group of people gives up their round booth to us. Apparently something was said by the huge tall guy. I don't know what it was but I do know that the guy I'm with just bought me yet another drink that I don't really need.

He is talking to one of the women about cooking classes. He writes the name of a cooking Web site on a card for her and shows it to me so I know he's not giving her his phone number or something.

"I don't care. I'm not possessive," I say.

Later that statement turns out to be so laughable it makes me want to cry.

"Are you going to put your arm around me again?" I say. He does.

Thursday, 11:30 p.m.

We're in a big conversation about writers. Maybe because I mentioned I am one, but I don't know. My memory is worse than my vision. We are talking about David Sedaris who is at Elliott Bay Books reading from *Dress Your Family in Corduroy and Denim* at that very moment. ("Let's go see him right now," he says. "I already called. It's sold out," I say.)

The guy in picture two recommends *Running with Scissors*, a book by another offbeat memoirist. He says he'll lend it to me, that like George from *Seinfeld* he feels the need to leave things with attractive women so they'll be forced to see him again. I give him my number and he programs it into his phone and it's kind of time to go.

Thursday, 11:00 p.m.

I'm sitting on the fringe of a big party sucking the pimiento out of the last olive in my martini and talking to my friend Ben about how much we both hate Bush. My girl friend appears and is taking pictures of some guy for a dating Web site.

"I'd go out with the guy in picture number two," I say, just to tease her since she's in "hostess mode." The truth is I have no idea what he looks like. I can't see three feet in front of me when I'm wearing my contacts, since they are off the rack and don't correct for my astigmatism. Of course he has heard us and immediately offers to buy me another martini and of course I let him.

I end up thinking of him as Teflon, since nothing I do sticks to him. He looks like a Dutch boy and has the kind of Hollywood features—a small, perfect triangle for a nose, overly big blue eyes, and a pouty lower lip—that would look great on television but look off balance in real life. He is cute close up. My eyesight is crap but my instincts are flawless.

TRUE CONFESSION

We were couple-y right away which is unusual for me and he was hands-y on the second date which is unusual for me to allow.

DATE 39   The Big Cheap

TRUE CONFESSION

The check lay there on the brown plastic thing that they sometimes put checks on. It was like a cigarette that some woman had tossed into the gutter and forgotten as soon as she lit another one. Maybe she was the kind of dame who doesn't pay for her own meals. I used to be that kind of dame and I would be again, but not tonight, sister, not tonight.

It was seven o'clock on Thursday night, late June. The early evening fog had turned Pike Market into a black-and-white photograph from the '50s. I didn't care about June or fog. I was trying to escape from men and dating and writing about men and dating.

I had had it with men. Had it up to here with their expensive dinners and not being sure of a commitment when I had already given them the best few weeks of my life. There was one man in particular who was causing me problems. He was the president. For the past four years he had been like a chronic yeast infection that all the Monistat in the world wouldn't cure. I wanted him out of office. I needed advice on how to get him out. That's all Anastasia knew, that's all she needed to know. Anastasia set this date up. She's got the number of every guy in town. And by that I mean she's literally got lots of guys' numbers in her Palm Pilot since she runs a social club. She set me up with Ira, a political consultant. I didn't know Ira, but I knew it wasn't too early to start thinking about the coming election. Not too early at all.

I walked past the pig statue in the market and I felt like it was mocking me, oinking at me. I started down the narrow, dank staircase when I heard someone following me. Then I realized it was the echo of my own heels against the cement.

I paused in the doorway of the Alibi Room. It was owned by tough-talking guys who knew all the lines. Lines from shows like *Northern Exposure,* because the actor who played Joel the doctor owns the place. He was pretty good in *Quiz Show.* Late at night the bar plays hip-hop music in the basement. It was still early and most people were just there to eat or have a drink and forget their problems and maybe find some new ones.

He was drinking a Manhattan at the bar. He looked like a younger Woody Allen, but with thinner hair. He *looked* like an Ira. "Are you Amy?" he said.

Who did he think he was kidding? He knew who I was. I was the only single dame in the place. I was wearing a skirt and black patent leather kitten-heeled shoes I'd bought at Value Village. I had straightened my hair and put on lipstick. I had just gotten off of the #18 bus and I didn't care who knew it.

I ordered a gin and tonic. We took a little table by the window.

To show him that I wasn't just some uptight feminist running a political campaign, I plucked the cherry out of his drink and lowered it into my mouth. It was the color of my lipstick.

"I wanted that," he said.

"Uh, I can get you another one from the bar."

"Well, I wanted that one."

"Sorry."

"It's just that the cherry's my favorite part."

The restaurant had the feel of a warehouse and it might have been one at one time. There was a window open over our heads, the kind that you pull down on a hinge like a drawbridge. Cigarette smoke from the couple behind us curled out of it like a lazy genie.

Ira ordered the morel risotto with asparagus. I ordered a chicken Caesar salad. I was running a political campaign but I didn't know anything about politics, although Caesar knew about politics and look where that got him.

I was calling my campaign Suffragette and the City. My plan was to get single women to vote and to get the president out of office.

"It's totally nonpartisan," I said. "I'm presenting it as having no other agenda than getting single women involved in the election."

"You're not fooling anyone," Ira said. "Getting single women to vote is just a front for getting votes for the Democrat, because that's the way those ladies swing. It's fine if you want to lie to me, or even lie to the American public, but don't lie to yourself. You should be *partisan*," he continued. "It shows passion."

"Like the passion you have for maraschino cherries?" I said.

He threw me off by changing the subject. "So are you going to write about me on your Web site?"

"I hadn't planned on it . . ."

"I'm newly separated. I've been married my whole adult life. I'm in my mid-thirties now. Dating has really changed."

"Oh, I bet it's hard," I said.

"No, I mean it's *great*. There are so many more women available to me now than there were when I was twenty-two."

I wondered if part of the reason single women weren't voting was because they were busy chasing guys like Ira? I felt like I should offer to pay for dinner since I was coming to him for advice. I was hoping he'd argue, that he'd somehow try to talk me out of it. I couldn't shake the feeling that I wasn't just paying for dinner, I was paying for taking that cherry. Ira was the kind of guy cherries seemed to matter to. I ended up picking up the check.

I decided to walk home. It had rained and the puddles were like mirrors. The signs of the weekly motel and the sex-toy shop made the sidewalk look like a neon pink watercolor on gray paper. Someone had scrawled "Curt + Corine" on a wall. Crazy kids, they would learn, or maybe they wouldn't.

As I was walking home a bum peed on my shoe. I gave him a quarter anyway.

DATE 40 Halloween in July

TRUE CONFESSION

I always think of this as The Night of Two Firsts (and, yes, they're the kind of firsts you might think).

I think I have a tarot-specific form of obsessive-compulsive disorder with astrological tendencies. I'm very superstitious, and often make up little rituals for myself, a trend that's only been exacerbated by years of living alone.

One of my favorite rituals is doing affirmations, which I repeat until I've whipped myself into a nervous frenzy of positive thoughts. Big, yet attainable goals are then subdivided into "written" and "spoken aloud." Sometimes I have so many affirmations going that they cancel one another out, for instance, "I'm with the perfect guy for me" seems to conflict with "I have a book deal based on dating tons of crazies." Somewhere mixed in there was "I will have a great boyfriend by the Fourth of July," which I had just remembered. I think it may have been a recycled one. I hate the Fourth of July. It's my least favorite holiday. I almost never have a good time. It seems like I'm always alone. (Those would be examples of nonpositive thoughts.)

Teflon builds supercomputers and always e-mails instead of calling. It was our third date.

He had given me my choice of the whole weekend and I picked

194

Saturday night. *Creative Visualization* says that sometimes if your goals don't manifest using affirmations, it may be that you feel conflicted about them. I wanted to spend the Fourth of July with a great boyfriend and yet I had picked July 3 to see Teflon, who I thought had the potential to be one. Spirituality is very complex.

We had just finished sharing a perfect meal of cashew chicken (something I order at every new Thai place so I can have an *x* factor when I do restaurant comparisons) and some beef and vegetables thing that he picked. We were at a little family-owned place a few blocks from my house.

"No fortune cookies," I said.

He threw a Visa down onto the check.

"Nope, just chocolates. Maybe your fortune is to travel to Peru," he said, passing me an Andes mint.

Next we went to an Irish pub that I don't care for, as it is always either silent as a tomb or crashed by people coming from sporting events wearing colored foam things on their heads. Although it was a weekend night, it was quiet for the time being.

Our whole excuse for getting together after we met at a party a few weeks before was so he could lend me *Running with Scissors*, a book he thought I'd like. I made some nice date chatter about it: "As a straight man, how did you feel about the graphic description of the thirteen-year-old boy being forced to give a blow job to his thirty-five-year-old neighbor?"

"I was fine with it. I definitely went through a homophobic period when I was younger, like in junior high, but now I couldn't care less."

I'm sure he was thrilled that I brought up the subject of blow jobs since he hadn't even been allowed into the lobby of my apartment building yet. I wanted to throw him off, though.

"Are you saying you're okay with statutory rape, then?"

"Well, no, of course not . . ."

"I like to think of myself as an amateur sociobiologist," I said. "I know we're not really tortoises, but in dating I think we do take our cues from Darwin."

"I agree. In fact I think we *are* tortoises at heart. It's just that we're the only species that has societal constraints on our mating."

"Those pesky statutory rape laws again?" I asked.

We talked about how even supposedly monogamous birds are found to have eggs fertilized by different males. This we both knew from the nature channel. He seemed a little too supportive of the theory that men have a biological responsibility to spread their seed. This was disturbing to me as I was really starting to like him. I wondered if Charles Darwin had been married, and, if so, how his theories went over with Mrs. Darwin.

"Would you like another beer?" The waitress reappeared.

I launched into a long explanation of how I wanted slightly less than a pint like they have at the alehouse at the top of the hill. The waitress and Teflon both looked confused. I gave up and ordered a whole pint.

"They know what I'm talking about at the top of the hill," I said after she left.

"Then you should definitely hang out there," he said.

As we were leaving he ran into some women he knew from work and laughed that the same thing had happened to him the night before. I could tell from his smugness that he had obviously been on a date then too.

There was an uncharacteristic chill in the air and it felt like October. We considered and then discarded the idea of sitting at the lookout at the top of the hill (where I'm understood) on the grounds that it was too cool. I suggested watching a video at my place, which of course he jumped at since that's guy-code for sex.

"Horror is my favorite genre," I said as we walked into the Blockbuster around the corner.

"Yeah, I like it a lot too. That and sci-fi."

"I dated a guy who was in this," I said picking up a copy of *Lake Badajuju: Part VII*. "He had a small but pivotal role."

"I didn't know the sixth sequel of a slasher movie could have a pivotal role."

A thin guy with a ponytail wearing a dark blue Blockbuster shirt and a name tag that said Mrs. Voorhees was stocking shelves. I picked up the DVD of *Halloween*.

"Do you know anything about the special features on this?" I asked him.

"Yes," he answered, and resumed stocking.

"What she means is, is this the one with special features or is that a different version?"

"It doesn't matter, I don't have a DVD player anyway," I said.

"Wow, that guy didn't like me," I said as Teflon and I walked back to my apartment with the VHS of *Halloween*. "I think it's because video store guys are all frustrated screenplay writers and get annoyed with people who know less about film than they do."

"I think it's that they have shitty jobs for just over minimum wage," he said.

"Do you know who Mrs. Voorhees is?" I said.

"Yes, she was the original killer in *Friday the 13th*. Before Jason. She was his mother."

I'm thrilled that he's able to draw upon horror-movie trivia. It's foreplay to me.

It was one of the only times in my life that I've been wildly physically attracted to someone who was actually solvent and educated and not crazy or on drugs. We were making out even before the teenagers in the movie were. I love kissing him. I love the way his lips feel on mine. I love that he's big and tall and not frail and little. Sociobiologists say that women are sexually drawn to men who have compatible blood types. I love his blood type I bet.

He ran his hand up my dress. After a while I dug my heel into his thigh so hard that he got a leg cramp.

"No one's ever been able to do that before," I said as he massaged his leg.

"I find that hard to believe. You're very . . . responsive."

"Do you want to go into my room?" I paused the film.

Teflon snapped me out of the haze that he had put me in by hesitating. "I guess we could . . ." he said.

I leaned back on my ivory down-feather comforter under a string of pink papier-mâché heart lights. He slid his hand down my leg to my foot, leaned on his elbows, and looked up at me. "Before we go any further, you should know that I have . . ."

Some horrible, communicable disease? A familial history of genocide that surfaces when he's aroused? I knew he was too good to be true.

". . . a fear of commitment."

"Oh. Wow," I said. I put a pillow under my head and looked at the ceiling. He moved up next to me and put his head on the other pillow.

"I first realized I had it after grad school. I could tell something was off. A lot of my friends were getting engaged and married but that just seemed like a lot to take on to me. I even lived with someone for five years."

"Did she ever catch it from you?"

"No," he said. "She met someone when we were together. After we broke up they got married right away. Marriage never came up in conversation when she and I were together, though."

"In five years?"

I didn't believe him. I suspected it was the disease talking.

"I don't mean to make you feel bad, but I'm kind of freaked out," I said.

"I've had lots of different reactions when I've told potential partners," he continued. "Everything from them breaking up with me to saying that they had it too."

"Well, I don't want to have sex unless we're at least committed to being exclusive," I said.

"That's okay. I'll just masturbate when I get home. That's what I usually do anyway."

As if to end the conversation he moved back down my body, slid his hands up my hips, and peeled my black lace boy-cut underwear off. "These are very sexy panties you're wearing," he said. He lowered his head. His tongue was agonizing. I arched into him and put my hands back over my head. If I'd had nails they would have dug into the wall. He gave me yet another first. Maybe this commitment thing was overrated.

It was late.

"I should go," he said, getting up to get his tennis shoes.

"Come here for a second," I said.

He had told me a secret and I remembered that I had one too. He lay back down beside me.

"This is weird, but . . . I write about my dates on the Internet. You're already on there. The thing is, it's really popular. I've been on the news. I'm even using it to run a political campaign."

He considered. "Well, thanks for telling me."

"I didn't want you to think I was just some unemployed person with nothing happening."

"I didn't think that," he said. "Hey, you should write about tonight and the two firsts. It's definitely something people should hear about."

"It's not that kind of a Web site," I said.

It was after midnight and I was alone. In the other room it was still Halloween and Jamie Lee Curtis remained on pause, frozen in a silent scream. Outside my bedroom window fireworks sparkled up over the hill, because it wasn't Halloween, it was the Fourth of July.

BUNK DEBUNK

Myth: The desire for commitment is a sexually transmitted disease.

Bunked!

It seems to affect women much more frequently than men, however. A woman can be tooling along, casually dating some guy, she's cool, maybe even a little aloof, nothing's a big deal, then . . . Bam! They start having sex and it's like someone turned on the faucet o' needy. Apparently orgasms release the chemical oxytocin—the substance that bonds a mother to her child also bonds formerly sane women to musicians and bikers.

One of my girl friends had invited me to a talk show called *Sex Live* that was being filmed at a club. The host was cute and tall and blond. The setting was relaxed and casual. He invited a woman he referred to as his "partner" onstage with him.

"I've never heard a man refer to a woman as his partner before," I whispered to my friend.

"It's because they're sex positive," she said.

"They've been tested for sex and they have one? They're positive they're not getting enough of it?" I said.

"No, they think sex is positive."

That makes me part of both the Food Positive and the Lying Around in Bed During the Day Reading Positive movements. And here I thought I wasn't a joiner.

Sex Positive movement. Hmph. Seems to me that it was yet another thing invented by men. All it meant was that everyone got to screw around and be honest about it, which is something not that many women desire anyway.

The guy who had invited my girl friend to the show

asked if she and I wanted to go for a drink afterward. He was good looking, very hip, well dressed, and charming. He had had his arm around a blonde girl all evening. He told us she was one of his secondary partners. As he said goodnight to her and left with my friend and me, I felt the pull, the hurt girlfriend pull—almost imperceptible—of seeing your "partner" (let's say it: lover, boyfriend, guy you hope you end up with) leave a club with other women. I saw it in her eyes.

At the bar my girl friend was drinking a key lime martini, the sexy guy was drinking a champagne and vanilla Stoli, and I was having a water because I wanted to keep a clear head in case I needed to extract myself from some sort of threesome scenario.

"So what's your deal with sex?" the sexy guy asked me when my friend was in the ladies' room.

"I'm done having fun, I want to get married," I said. He nodded understandingly as if I weren't joking.

"Was that blonde girl you were with your girlfriend?" I asked.

"No. God no, if I were really into someone I wouldn't want her coming to parties like these. I'd be home with her."

I knew it. Positively.

DATE 41 "I Saw Your Name over a Urinal in Tacoma . . ."

TRUE CONFESSION

When I accepted this dinner invitation from Date 15, a man I had dated last year, I was completely preoccupied by the guy from Dates 37, 38, and 40. My guilt was eased when I found out that on our previous date he had been completely preoccupied by some woman who didn't have a number.

I already felt like things had moved way too quickly with Teflon, with the pseudo sex (depending on your definition) and the conversation about his commitment phobia, which may or may not have been triggered by him not liking me that much. I decided that since I liked him so much, the best course of action would be to break up with him. I did so by e-mail. Of course secretly I hoped he would try to talk me out of it. I've always heard that the best way to get your mind off obsessing about a particular man is to date a different one, so I did that too.

I had recently gotten a mention in the *Seattle Times,* so I was not at all surprised when one of my former dates e-mailed. I was, however, surprised that he asked me out again. He is the guy from TV, a blind date I went to a super-spicy Thai lunch with a year and a half ago—the same day I did the morning radio interview with those two Howard Stern–like DJs from Detroit—and then never heard from again. After reading my date report on the Web site (where I said that he never called), he sent an e-mail: "I really didn't think you had any interest in me from our Thai lunch, although you had definitely piqued my interest."

Since he had spelled *piqued* correctly, I decided to meet him for dinner at an Indian place. The real reason he hadn't asked for a second date the year before came out before the onion naan: he was using my own strategy on me. Not the one where you break up with someone you like, but the one where you date someone to get your mind off of someone else. Apparently he had met a woman a few days before our first date, but thought it would be rude to cancel on me. They had been dating ever since. She had recently gone back to an ex-boyfriend and TV was back in the showroom.

I ordered a chardonnay. As I tore off a piece of warm bread and dipped it in mint sauce, the second bit of truth came out: he hadn't seen my Web site in the *Seattle Times* after all. "I don't know if you're going to like this, but I saw the name of your site in a bathroom in Tacoma."

I couldn't say I was completely surprised. I had certainly asked for it to be scrawled on men's-room walls. I was grateful more people didn't have my number, actually.

"I was at a restaurant breaking up with that woman I dated and I saw one of your postcards with the red Dating Amy logo over a urinal," he said.

While not as bad as "For a good time call . . ." it was certainly odd, since I don't have postcards for my Web site.

I must have looked like I just bit into a lemon. "Don't feel bad, it was right up there with the postcards for Skyy vodka and Toblerone. I made a mental note to look up your site when I got home—it's such a great name. I recognized your picture and then I recognized our date."

Apparently my career and my love life were both in the toilet.

Maybe I shouldn't have been so hasty with my breakup/ploy for attention with Teflon. I wondered if he had seen my e-mail yet? My answer to the future of my budding/dead relationship could be waiting for me in my inbox even as I pulled apart my chicken tiki. Anxiety was setting in.

TV had ordered the Indian version of a chicken and rice casserole and he was continuing his story of the toilet-paper trail I had left.

"I saw that you had been on a talk show with my network, so I went into the archives and watched the tape. You didn't look like yourself at all."

Thank God. He was referring to the Captain Kirk interview.

As TV was watching the tape, the host of the show walked by and he told her he had dated me.

She said that Penny, my friend with the leaving-her-husband Web site, was weird.

"Did she think I was weird?" I asked.

"Probably, but she didn't say so since I said I knew you."

Huh.

After dinner we went for coffee and my curiosity/dread about Teflon was starting to overflow. I knew at this point that he was probably feeling like he had dodged a bullet since the weird dating chick had made things easier and ended it first. I was so distracted that I was beyond the point of polite conversation with TV.

I finished my latte in record time and invited him to a party where we would both be able to meet other people to help us get over our recent and future breakups.

I ran home and logged onto my e-mail account.

There were no new messages.

DATE 42 Awkward Positions, Sexual and Otherwise

TRUE CONFESSION

I feel like the undignified half of the couple, as if I'm flailing around to get the attention of the other person like a drowning swimmer to a lifeguard, Lucy to Schroeder or Arnold Horshack to Mr. Kotter.

The next morning I got a response to my breakup e-mail. "Hi, Amy, Sorry it took me a while to get back to you. I wanted to think about this. I do like you. I want to see where this goes. If you're going to Anastasia's party, I'll buy you a drink."

A friend of mine was telling me that her ex-boyfriend's favorite sexual position is similar to the plow position in yoga. It's like lying on your back with your legs flung over your head and just your shoulders and toes touching the ground with your nose pointed at your belly button, curled up like a shrimp, midway through a somersault. He'd be on top, hammering down.

"Is it any wonder he still calls me three years after the breakup? There aren't many women out there as dumb as I am."

"No, no, you're fun and adventurous!" I said, thinking, *There's no way I'd let someone do that with me.*

For the past month Teflon had been putting me into a different kind of unnatural position. The position of not getting my own way, the position of not having the upper hand, the position of caring more than he does. While he viewed me utterly casually, I viewed him as a combination of Brad Pitt and Jimmy Stewart. Although objectively he is clearly neither, chemicals had flooded my brain and I could not see or think clearly.

Apparently a secondary effect of those chemicals is that they attract a whole lot of other men. TV and I met on the corner and walked over to the party Anastasia was throwing at a bar near my house.

He was getting me a martini when I heard someone say, "Amy." It was Eric Van Halen, the writer I had dated a few times in March when my interest level went from Yay!-he-took-my-number-he-is-the-only-man-here-I-want to I'm-not-calling-him-back. I don't know what happened exactly, except that it seemed closely related to him liking me too much and me being forced to walk long distances in heels.

He had cut off his long hair and seemed happy to see me. We chatted with a group of his guy friends and he recommended a seminar he heard about called "Why the Hell Does No One Want to Publish My Book?" I finally extracted myself because TV didn't know a soul there and was holding my martini as conversation collateral.

TV was telling me a story about how he met Angelina Jolie when she was up here filming a movie where she played a platinum blonde newscaster. He said she had an oddly shaped face. I guess it's possible that the kindness of the camera lens makes her look like the most ungodly beautiful woman in the world. Works for me. He was really only on a dinner break from work, so he finished his Long Island iced meal and left.

A half hour later Eric caught up with me again.

"I'm sorry about how I left things before," I said. "I shouldn't have just not returned your calls. I handled things badly."

"It's okay," he said. He sounded like he meant it. "I'm not seeing anyone now. And I've also become a Buddhist." He did look peaceful. I was almost convinced he wasn't interested in me until I caught him smelling my hair.

He asked me out for that weekend "just to hang out" and I accepted.

As he had promised, Teflon was at the party too. I had just made a date with the fifth guy who had asked me out that night when I thought I would go over and say hello. He was surrounded by a group of women. He was buying rounds of drinks for everyone as usual. When I say I'm crazy about him, unfortunately I mean it literally.

"Do you want me to get a chair so you can sit down?" he asked.

"No. I won't bother you while you're holding court," I said, and stormed off.

It's like science fiction. An entity has taken over my body. The words come out of my mouth, but I don't recognize them as anything I would say. Ever.

We've had three dates, two make-out sessions, and several fights. The problem, ironically given my career path, is that I want us to date exclusively and he doesn't. I couldn't be more uncomfortable if my neck were at a ninety-degree angle to my mattress with my legs flung over my head.

He caught up with me at the bar.

"Are you okay?"

"Yes. I'm fine."

"You don't seem fine. You seem like you're pissed. Because I'm socializing. At a party."

I was armed with mixed metaphors and questionable statistics.

"Well, you're over there with a fucking harem. Like a king with a harem. Don't you know that the ratio in Seattle is supposed to favor women, not men, by something like three to one? Am I supposed to be some sort of harem jester who's only coming in at one . . . third?"

"Sorry, but this is really flattering. I'm a computer-science major. We don't have women react to us like this."

"I just . . . I don't want us to see other people."

"I'm not comfortable with that. And we've already had problems. I have a good time with you and physically, I think . . ." He looked at the ground. "Physically . . . I love making out with you. But I can't read you. The second time we went out you barely said two words to me at dinner. I thought you didn't want to be with me. I like to be able to read someone instantly," he said.

"If you've connected with people so immediately before, then why aren't you still with any of them?"

"Things just didn't work out."

"Is an instant connection what usually happens to you?"

"No, usually things start out this way," he said, indicating me. "Ninety-five percent of the time anyway."

"This is a great conversation," I said.

"I know, it's visceral," he said happily. We were like actors breaking character.

We argued about our three-date-old relationship for almost an hour. I learned that he was willing to talk about his commitment problem. I learned that he doesn't think we don't have a future. I learned that if you talk about wanting to kiss the hidden tattoos of the beautiful Asian woman tending bar you can get a guy to forget all about harems and walk you home.

"Do you want to come in?" I said when we reached the door to my building.

"It was implied in the invitation to walk you home."

I tripped over one of his tennis shoes in the entryway when I came out of the bathroom. He always takes his shoes and watch off if he's expecting some action. I got us individual bottles of water and sat next to him on the couch.

"Got your watch off, I see," I said. "Should I light candles?"

"I don't know. I want to go in there," he said, looking at my room.

"You don't like my couch?" I was a bit offended. My couch is a pale-olive-green-and-cream paisley, overstuffed and gorgeous. I paid a month's salary for it once upon a time.

"I like the couch, but I've already been in the bedroom," he said. Men see almost everything as a hierarchy. Of course the couch seemed like a step backward to him. In my room he had both of our clothes off in less than four seconds.

"I'm not so sure about this," I said. He was hovering over me.

He pushed into me a little.

"I don't think you'll fit." I was remembering the Christmas Tree incident.

"It's 'cause you're resisting."

He pushed in again, a little deeper this time.

"Cut it out. This is totally not safe sex."

"Well, better get a condom then."

By "safe" I had meant emotionally. It still bothered me—especially bothered me—that we didn't have a definite commitment.

"I love your body," I said.

"Wow, you can say that after seeing me naked?"

I mentioned the tattooed Asian bartender again, this time casting myself as the lead in the scenario as the faux resistance on my part fell away.

"Are you trying to get something going?" It was the next morning and he was biting my neck.

"Yes, I guess I was."

"I need coffee," I said, pushing him off.

"You seem so innocent. Maybe not innocent but . . . you're not though." He was talking to himself, looking at the ceiling and playing with his own chest hair. "Icon Grill and Viceroy . . ." He was referring to the pretty restaurant and hip little bar where we had our second date. "I should have taken you to Thirteen Coins diner and Five Corners . . . what's that awful dive?"

"Five Points Saloon?" I yelled from the kitchen.

"Yeah, Five Points. That place is so bad."

He was over at the near edge of the bed. I put my coffee down and curled into the sliver of space next to him.

"If I had brought *you* home spontaneously, I don't know if my place would have been this clean," he said. "I want you to see my house. I think it looks good—I have little accents around and stuff. What are you doing for dinner on Friday night? I could cook. Any dietary restrictions? I think I'll make pork loins with garlic mashed potatoes and some sort of seasonal vegetable. Maybe flash-broiled asparagus. I'll go to Pike Market."

"Okay," I said. I was thrilled. He was obviously not freaked out that we had had sex.

He resumed neck biting.

"Now I'm a big slut for picking you up at a party," I said later.

He was pulling on his jeans. "I know! And I get to be a stud. It's so unfair."

I put on a black Gap tank top and black drawstring shorts and walked him to the door.

"Don't tell the guys at work about me," I said. He looked bemused and didn't answer. "Not the ones I know at least," I said as he turned to go down the stairs.

There aren't many women out there as dumb as I am, but at least he didn't put me in some sort of plow position.

Five Points Saloon, though. Bastard.

BUNK DEBUNK

Myth: You can tell what a man's like in bed by how he spends his money.

Bunked!

The ancient Greeks believed that love and money were both ruled by the same goddess—Venus. According to my not-so-ancient girl friends, they were right. As you know if you've dated a miserly rich guy, generosity is more important than assets. Speaking from personal experience, if you get asked out by a starving artist and are hesitant to date him because he had to put your eggs and toast on his Visa (yet refused to let you go Dutch), well, his FICO score is probably not the only thing that's constantly going down.

DATE 43 Pork Loins and Pointy Ears

TRUE CONFESSION

I learned that you should never do a rewrite about going to bed angry.

Sir Isaac Newton said that every action has an opposite and equal reaction.

I interpret that to mean that the less I do for men, the more they do for me. It made sense that since the only thing I've served him at my apartment is water, Teflon wanted to cook me a beautiful dinner at his house.

Our communication is mostly by e-mail and I flirted in writing that I was going to wear my Sophia Loren shoes—three-inch '50s-style Italian pumps I can't walk in.

He said, "I can't wait to see them, but don't expect to do too much walking."

At the last minute I was gripped by some sort of bipolar modesty that caused me to choose lower heels but to wear a low-cut, skintight black dress.

He picked me up at six on the dot—always at six on the dot, actually. I love it that he's always on time.

"Let's see the shoes," he said.

"I was too shy to wear them."

He kissed me.

I peeked into the backseat at the dinner groceries from Pike

212

Market. No flowers, even though there are women hawking bouquets every three feet there. I don't care about flowers, I was just desperate for a clue as to how he felt about me.

On the drive over we made small talk—infinitesimal talk, really—about traffic patterns. His house is in one of those gorgeous Seattle hillside neighborhoods and his yard is anchored by an ancient, weeping tree.

I think cooking dinner together is a way for a couple to bond and get to know each other. For my contribution I perched on the counter, immediately had too much chardonnay, rambled on in non sequiturs, and didn't slide off the Formica until the food was ready.

As promised, dinner was pork loins, really some of the best garlic mashed potatoes I've ever had, flash-broiled asparagus, salad, and yet more wine.

After dinner he let me choose a DVD. I went to the wall in his basement and returned with a copy of *The Shining*.

"It was the only thing I could find that didn't have to do with *Star Trek*," I said.

"I don't have *Star Trek*. It hasn't been released on DVD, yet," he said, gearing up for what I was sure would be a frightening, technical explanation about things I don't care to know that he knows.

"I saw the whole *Babylon 5* series down there . . ." I said as if describing decomposed bodies I'd discovered under the floorboards.

"*Babylon 5* isn't *Star Trek*."

We watched *The Shining* (umpteenth time for both of us certainly) and drank white wine and ate chocolate and lemon cookies from the Italian grocer. We were locked in each other's arms when I looked over his shoulder and saw that he had stopped the DVD player at the moment where the dead, naked woman from the bathtub is locked in Jack Nicholson's arms.

"Ew, sweetie, can you . . ." He shut it off.

Upstairs he lit candles all around his bedroom.

"Hurry up. Come to bed," I said after he had burned himself about three times.

"You *are* a brat," he said as he came into my arms. "How limber are you?"

Nightfall comes late in the Pacific Northwest in the summer. I could still hear the neighbor kids playing outside.

"Are you sleepy?" I asked after a few hours.

"No," he said.

"Do you want to go finish the movie?" I said.

We went back downstairs. He was wearing just a shirt.

"You're not going to put on pants?" I said.

"Given the past three hours it seemed kind of . . . formal."

I wouldn't want someone sitting naked on my couch, I don't think, but his couch had an ugly dark-brown-and-orange geometrical pattern that it would be silly to baby. It was an earth-toned blotch in the rest of an absolutely beautiful two-story house. The main floor had no walls. The living room was one big cream-colored expanse that flowed into his well-used kitchen.

The next morning I lay around in his bed while he got ready to go play tennis.

"You bought this house five years ago?"

"Yeah, I bought it with a girlfriend and she moved out six months later . . . you probably don't want to hear about past girlfriends."

"It's okay."

I was more disturbed that he was getting ready to meet a "friend" for tennis that morning and was going to the symphony "with people from work" that night. I suspected they were both dates.

I was trying to remind myself that we really hadn't known each other that long when he gave me my very own toothbrush. It was blue. I thought it was a gift and started to put it in my purse. "If you bring it home, you have to remember to bring it back," he said. "You only get one. It's meant for you to leave here."

He has been adamant about seeing other women. He has told me in so many words that I'm not right for him. I wanted to tell him it was cruel to lead me on by keeping something for me at his house, but instead I just said, "I'll leave it here, but at least put my name on it."

BUNK DEBUNK

Myth: *Sex too early can ruin a promising relationship*.

Debunked!

I'm not a big fat slut, but some of my guy friends and girl friends are, so I brought this one up with the not-always-thinking-with-their-brain trust. After a very careful and measurable analysis, I have come to the scientific conclusion that there is no correlation between having sex right away and the failure of the relationship. On the other hand if you *do* have sex right away and the other person later breaks up with you, I guess sex is as good a scapegoat as any, with the added bonus that it makes the other person look like a hypocrite or a puritan depending on how you spin it.

DATE 44   A Bad First Impressionist

TRUE CONFESSION

I was bummed that Eric Van Halen invited me to something expensive that I wouldn't have gone to otherwise and then asked me to pay my own way. There's a reason great art is described as priceless, though.

I was thrilled when Eric Van Halen called—thrilled to have a distraction. I had reconnected with him at the same party I ended up leaving with Teflon.

We made another attempt at the art museum. Our first try last spring had to be aborted due to the fact that we arrived two hours past closing time.

When he picked me up he was wearing a black Big Star T-shirt and jeans and his hair was slicked back. He is half Latin and it was his best hair look yet.

I felt off center. For one thing my date with Teflon had been the night before and I had just gotten out of bed with him eight hours earlier. It felt funny to be out with another man so soon. I want to be cool and free-spirited about dating, but I'm just not. It's like dark red aspiring to be powder blue or telling an impressionist to be more realistic.

There was also the inevitable comparison. Eric had told me beforehand how much the tickets to the exhibit cost, so I was clued in that I was to pay my own way. Teflon would never let a woman—

216

me or any of those other bimbos, as I thought of them—pay her own way on a date. He didn't even let people pay for drinks when they were sitting at his table during parties, but instead opened a tab at the bar and acted as a combination drink runner–benefactor of alcohol to everyone. I was feeling miffed because it wasn't an exhibit I would have seen—and thus paid for—on my own. It was a Dutch woman's private collection and the big draw was that there were some van Goghs included. I've been to the van Gogh Museum in Amsterdam, though, and really, what's more van Gogh than that? This would be a step down by definition. I was already feeling shortchanged both monetarily and artwise.

But it was amazing.

Rather than rent those headsets that have an expert explaining what the paintings signify, I relied on Eric's commentary.

"You can really see how the impressionists influenced the middle period of Whitesnake's album covers," he said, contemplating a piece with naked chicks entwined with serpents.

He also knew a bit about art history:

"Part of the reason van Gogh died so young was from paint fumes."

"I thought it was because he put a gun to his head and pulled the trigger," I said.

"Well, that too, but the fumes didn't help."

When van Gogh was younger he was an art dealer. His drawings at that time were very realistic and plain. Our last stop was a whole room reserved for his later work, the work he is known for, the work he did when his insanity became as bright as his palette. Even against the lilies and dots of Monet and Seurat, his paintings were male peacocks spreading their fans in a roomful of brown hens. It made me wonder whether there really is something more appealing about being crazy. Perhaps it explains my success with men—my success with attracting them at least.

Afterward, Eric took me to a park. In the simmering heat of the evening I felt like I was in the muted colors of an impressionist painting. The park was sculpted by the designer of Central Park. The city was in the distance and I saw the Space Needle as I've never seen it. A troupe was doing Shakespeare in the Park as I've also never seen it: in business casual.

Of course at one point I did have to climb up a muddy slope in heels, but this time I wanted Eric Van Halen to help keep me steady in them by holding my hand.

Later that week, I was in a blissful haze/complete nervous panic over Teflon. I felt a lot closer to him after the dinner at his house. Every word of his, every action, took on a crucial quality.

It was Friday and he had casually asked me out for Sunday night and even qualified it by saying he had to be up early the next day. Well of course he had to be up early, the next day was Monday. I couldn't believe he wasn't asking me for Saturday night. It even highlighted one of the Bunk Debunks on my Web site, which said that if you're not getting Saturday nights with someone, you're strictly second string.

"I'll pass on the glamorous Sunday night offer," I said. "I have to start taking my own advice sometime."

"I'm a bit mystified about the whole Saturday night thing," he said. "I don't tend to value one night over any other and find the string comment, well, odd. I understand that there may be an underlying sentiment, let's just not dress it up in some arbitrary veneer of what night we go out on. That's just too confusing to me."

I had stupidly gushed about how great our date at his house was on the Web site. It would be best to salvage some dignity and change the write-up, I thought. In part I changed it to:

We are different, he and I. He planned the menu a week ahead of time. I don't know if I'll be in Amsterdam this time next week. He asked if I have any dietary restrictions. Not only do I not have any, but I don't even say things like "dietary restrictions."

"I don't have *Star Trek*. It hasn't been released on DVD, yet," he said, gearing up for what I was sure would be a frightening, technical explanation of things I would never want to hear from someone I've let touch me. It couldn't be more frightening than the pattern on his ugly brown-and-orange couch, however.

Jesus. Why not just put on an overly tight blue shirt with a little black insignia on it, fashion some wax ear points, and be done with it? Am I at a fucking convention?

We settled in to watch something far less disturbing: Jack Nicholson going insane at a snowbound hotel and slaughtering his family.

I was a little angry.

BUNK DEBUNK

Myth: If you're not getting Saturday night dates, you're second string.

Bunked!

It doesn't mean he/she doesn't like you, doesn't mean you smell or dress funny, doesn't mean you're a bad person, and *definitely* doesn't mean I'm a bad person for telling you, but if you're not together on Date Night, they're either cruising for someone else or dating someone they like better. I will consider rebuttals, but only if your heart's desire works in a bar and Tuesday nights *are* his Saturday nights or something.

DATE 45 Harry Potter and the Fish of Rubber

TRUE CONFESSION

Harry Potter is one of the most interesting men I've ever met.

Harry Potter is cute and dark and slender. Harry Potter wears a wool newsboy cap. Harry Potter drives a very old car that has seat belts more suited to an amusement park ride than something you would depend upon should you come into abrupt contact with another vehicle. He is an artist and a fiddle player and a conspiracy theorist. We have seen each other probably half a dozen times since we've met. He is very funny.

Sometimes if the weather's beautiful I wait for my dates outside. I sit on the stoop and stretch my legs and watch people passing by with their dogs—plastic bag in one hand, leash in the other.

I know when Harry is coming a mile away though, so I just run downstairs when I hear the distant cry of his not-so muffler.

"I'm sorry I'm late. I was passing a yard sale at the top of the hill and this guy was just giving me all this great stuff."

I looked in the backseat to see a bag of dirt and a used tent.

It was one of those astonishing Seattle evenings: warm, sunny, perfect.

"I was thinking we could go someplace and sit outside," he said.

When we got to the restaurant with the patio on the water we realized that the rest of Seattle had had the exact same idea, but forty-five minutes earlier. The lobby was packed with people waiting for a seat outdoors, but the Meg Ryan–at–twenty-one hostess chirped that she could seat us right away. Inside. Near the kitchen.

"I can't do this," said Harry. "I know another place."

Then he spoke words I'm learning to dread from any of my dates: "We'll walk. It's not that far."

The gravel between the railroad tracks crunched under the chunky platform heels of my sandals. We walked past a home where someone had rolled a red caboose off the tracks and into their backyard. It had a waterfall of yellow flowers spilling out of it.

"You miss so much when you're driving," Harry said. I miss bits of conversation and most of what's on the radio when Harry is driving because I can't hear a thing over the roar of his engine but I didn't say so.

"I used to ride the rails," he said. "You jump on a car when it stops in your city and just go wherever. It's a cheap way to travel. Some of the people you end up sharing a car with can be kind of scary, but after not showering for a while, you fit right in."

"Did you actually sleep in the car surrounded by people you didn't know?" I said. I can't sleep if my neighbor across the alley turns on the light in her bedroom because she doesn't draw her blinds and it subtly shines through mine, so the thought of being relaxed enough to sleep next to desperate, crazy strangers in a moving freight car fascinates me.

"Well, you don't 'not know them' for long. There was a guy I met named Speedy—because of his drug of choice. He made me a little nervous because you don't necessarily want to travel with a guy like that, especially since he carried a gun. You can't let them know you're an outsider or you'll get jumped. You have to drink cheap alcohol and minimize your vocabulary."

This makes sense to me since it's how I've managed my writing career so far.

"You definitely don't want them to think you're like some college-educated art-school poseur who's just jumping trains for fun."

"But you were."

"I know, but you don't want a guy named Speedy to know that. The friend I traveled with couldn't even wear his expensive watch."

Harry and I reached our destination: a cute restaurant on the water where the party was in full swing and the clientele was all of the same nationality. It was obviously somebody's wedding. Beautiful dark-haired children ran around the gleaming wooden floor. Couples danced the tango and waiters carried trays of champagne. I could see the water through the distant picture window and realized how hungry I was when I felt envy for a wasp that flew in and landed on some canapés.

"Do you think they'd notice if we just went in and grabbed some food and a glass of champagne?" I said, not really kidding. Harry looked down at his jeans and Tevas. "Yeah, I think they would." He seemed a little horrified. Sure, he can hop on freight trains and not shower and play the harmonica or what have you with speed freaks who carry weapons, but crashing a wedding for a few minutes with me is out of the question.

We ended up farther down the tracks, even metaphorically. "Well I didn't think I'd be here tonight, but it is a Seattle institution I guess," he said as we approached a little dive near the locks.

Outside summer was in her full glory; inside it looked like a perpetual last call. We took a corner booth near a tiny open window. Harry let me sit in front of the box fan that was trying to suck a trickle of fresh air into the hot, smoky room. I ordered fish and chips and a chardonnay and shamed him into changing his order from just salad to breaded fried fish and salad since the place claims to have World Famous Fish and Chips and why would they lie?

At the first restaurant Harry had run into someone he knew (not Speedy), so I asked about the guy.

"We both used to hang out at this place in the U District called The Last Exit," he said.

Apparently yet another Seattle institution, it used marble splash guards taken from urinals as tables.

"There was a woman there who thought she was a witch. She would flick her fingers at us from across the room and we'd turn to our friends and say, 'Witch Evie just cast a spell on me and I don't know what it is.'"

"Maybe it's that you can never drive a car younger than you?" I said.

We ate our fish and chips and salad. I soaked my fries in catsup and we were honest and checked "rubbery" on the How Was Your Fish? comment card they had at the table next to the vase of wilting daisies.

I wanted to go to the coffee shop that was showing Harry's paintings. I had never been there before. It had a gorgeous winding staircase and was connected to an old-time movie theater that put cumin on its popcorn.

They let Harry keep a carton of vanilla ice cream in their freezer since he's a regular. He asked for two scoops of it, plus an orange soda and two straws so he could make us an orange-cream float to share. I looked around at his paintings and was taken aback, not just because they were good, but because they were normal. I could see these paintings in anyone's home or office. No wonder people were offering $700 a pop for them. He had told me they were really dark. I was picturing skeletons, dismembered bodies, witches—perhaps a portrait of Evie. Apparently by *dark* he meant the actual color scheme. Well, there was one dismembered torso in a baking pan, but even that would look great in someone's kitchen.

For the first time that night we got a table outside.

"I'm totally corporate with my art," he said when I expressed my surprise at what I can only describe as his commercialism. "I'm not like artists where this splotch represents man's struggle with God or something. I just go with what looks good. It's because I have no soul."

Harry Potter has no money. Harry Potter has no muffler. But as we sat on the patio under the midnight-blue night sky surrounded by white fairy lights and ate the orange floats he'd made for us, I couldn't agree that Harry Potter has no soul.

Harry Potter and the
Enchanted Barbecue

TRUE CONFESSION

Harry Potter's friends are some of the funniest people I've
ever met.

Once upon a time I wanted to be a singer. And a songwriter.
And a guitar player. I ended up as a writer. And an underground
Internet celebrity. And poor. I was selling equipment from the
first career to support the second, and Harry Potter was my knight
in salvaged armor. He had introduced me to his friend Todd, who
was going to buy my Fender Blues Deluxe, a tweed tube amp that
is the stuff musicians' dreams are made of.

The beautiful late August Sunday afternoon was slanting
toward evening. Todd invited us to a barbecue at his house on the
other side of the hill. I mashed some ripe avocados and mixed
them with *pico de gallo* while Harry talked to me in the kitchen
and Todd sang a made-up narration for *Six Feet Under,* which he
was watching with the sound on mute. We vibrated up the hill in
Harry's car with Todd lying on the folded-down backseat hugging
his new amp.

We stopped by a little grocery store and Todd gave Harry money
to get us a six-pack of imported beer. It was only $3.49 and again I

was struck by how poor Harry is . . . he actually asked for the money. Todd was like a father handing over an allowance.

I have about one cigarette every six months and I was due, so I smoked in the parking lot with Todd while we waited for Harry.

"You should join our band," said Todd.

"I'm not much of a singer."

"You'll fit right in, we're not much of a band. We need a woman around. Women elevate the level of everything."

"That was the problem with bands I was with in the past."

"Yeah, all problems with men can be traced back to one thing: the penis."

"I'm a straight woman and you're telling me this? How did you meet your wife?" I said.

"We were both working for a music company. She was this older woman and when I saw her . . . that was it for me. I'm insanely attracted to her."

"That's so nice to hear. Did you just get married?"

"Nah, we've been together twenty years."

When we got back to Todd's house he and his not-so-new bride immediately got into a fight in the house while Harry and I sat on the patio.

"Should we leave?" I said. "I bet they're arguing because he made some sort of unilateral decision. Men are good at that."

"You guys, I get nervous when Mom and Dad fight," Harry yelled into an open window. "Are you getting a divorce?"

Todd came out and joined Harry and me on the patio. "No, I just made a unilateral decision about where we're grilling and didn't consult her," he said. I knew it.

Todd and his wife live in a tiny, darling Craftsman-style house with a small garden patio surrounded by tall pines. Harry had been painting and designing the interior for the past six weeks. "Can you finish it soon, by the way? I'd like to have sex with my wife this month and she's holding out until you're done," said Todd.

Their next-door neighbor Sam was the inspiration for the barbecue. He had bought buffalo burgers from a roadside store on his way back from Montana. A guitar teacher by trade, he had taken off by himself for a week of camping and fly-fishing.

He was probably twenty-four, cute, and bookish looking with straight blond hair and glasses. "It was incredible. I didn't see anyone for days. I got sunburned all over because I was naked most of the time," he said. "Then as I was leaving I accidentally backed over my little backpacker guitar with my truck. I didn't like it that well anyway, so I just left it there."

"Running over a guitar you don't like is like putting Grandma on an ice floe," said Todd.

He picked up his acoustic guitar and started to narrate in song like he had done at my apartment:

> Grandma . . . we can't afford to feed you anymore
> Get a load of this ice floe
> Say hello to the narwhals
> We love you
> Good-bye

We had my guacamole, the grilled buffalo burgers and grilled white corn, butter lettuce salad with honey-mustard dressing. When we ran out of the beer Harry had bought and Todd had paid for, we switched to white wine.

It was dark now. Todd's wife brought out white candles and French dessert wine and a lilac pashmina for me to wear because the night chill was setting in. She was tall and willowy with long hair, like a cross between a hippie and an elegant French woman.

". . . Harry and I have a symbiotic relationship, he drives and I pay for things," Todd was saying.

I told them that when I was in second grade I wrote a science paper on symbiosis, the tendency of certain animals to form beneficial relationships with animals of a different species. God, even as a seven-year-old I was fascinated with writing about relationships, I realized.

"You were the talk of the teachers' lounge I bet," said Todd. "Other kids were writing about a squirrel in their backyard and you bust out a paper on symbiosis."

"Yeah," said Harry. "'I saw a squirrel in my backyard. I fed it some nuts. It had a furry tail. I like squirrels. The end.'"

"The other kids were seven, not retarded, Harry," I said.

"It's not retarded, I've heard worse political acceptance speeches: 'I am Mayor Nickels. I am the mayor of Seattle. The police chief doesn't like me. I like Seattle. The end.'"

"I have a song about Harry," said Todd. "It's about your car and your Dumpster diving. I call it 'The Bravest Scrounger in All the Land.'"

"Oh God, that's it. I can't take it. I'm buying a Mercedes tomorrow," said Harry.

"Sam, I want to hear you play," I said to the neighbor.

"Yeah, get your guitar."

While Todd is as unique in song as he is in life, with his comic, nasal voice and naughty, brilliant stream-of-consciousness lyrics—Harry swears he's a genius—Sam writes my kind of songs: catchy, brief, pure sugar pop.

He commanded us to be his slutty backup singers and we sang along as his chorus until the white candles melted into stubs and the white stars came out in legion.

DATE 47 Eric Van Halen and the Regular Barbecue

TRUE CONFESSION

Sometimes the most important way to decide what kind of relationship you want is to see the kind you don't want.

"Do you relate to femininity at all?" a girl with glittery butterfly clips in her hair asked Patti Smith. It sounded like an accusation.

"I like the way Jeanne Moreau smokes or the way certain women can wear a black sweater and look amazing," the older woman answered. "I guess I'm not quite sure what you mean."

Whatever the girl with butterflies meant, it wasn't that. She had acrylic nails, for God's sake. There were two very different intellectual levels going on here and the twain weren't meeting. It was an interesting question, though.

We already knew Patti Smith related to masculinity: Her anecdotes included some of the most interesting men of the '60s. "Allen and Bob convinced me to come back to music in 1996. Years later I took my daughter to Allen's deathbed. I wanted her to see a peaceful death. She ate the cookies the monks had left for the gods. William was calling constantly. It was an amazing experience and not just for my daughter."

Allen and Bob were Ginsberg and Dylan. The William who was ringing the phone off the hook was Burroughs.

That's my kind of femininity: the ability to get extraordinary, creative men buzzing around you like an illustrious hive.

Eric Van Halen and I were at a small in-store performance. I hated myself for agreeing a little with Butterfly Bimbo's implied criticism of the show when she and her friends left after about fifteen minutes. Maybe like me they were hoping that Patti Smith would scorch through "Because the Night," but she was hell-bent on talking politics.

A few miles and light-years of consciousness away, Eric and I were planning on a picnic on Mercer Island with a friend of his— a childhood friend who had become a high-powered lawyer— and his new wife, Ellen, whom Eric hadn't met yet. On the way to the island, I thought about my own definition of femininity. I settled on being an antebellum feminist: traditional about chivalry, the men paying and opening doors, but then being as outspoken as I want to be while collecting a paycheck equal to any man's.

Eric seemed to have his own definition of femininity going on that day. Not only did he stop and ask for directions, but he had to borrow my cell phone to call his friends. The cooler he brought to the barbecue was completely empty; I didn't think he was much of a provider.

When we got to his friend's apartment, a new definition of masculinity surfaced: heightened. The lawyer and Eric talked about a specific hockey game from years ago for literally forty-five minutes. The worst part was I had already heard the excruciating story on a previous date with him. Another couple joined us—she worked at Starbucks, not the corporation, but at an actual coffee place, and he was sort of a supremely intelligent long-haired liberal. I was surprised that the obviously Republican lawyer would be friends with the liberal, or with Eric, for that matter. It was quite a party—even the dips had genders: chopped tomatoes with onion and basil and crostini for the women, sour cream and beans and a thick layer of American cheese with potato chips for the men.

On our first date, Eric had told me that his life was like *The Man Show*. I saw a little more of what he meant when after the mind-numbing discussion about the Hockey Game, the liberal and the lawyer began to discuss politics. Arguing doesn't bother me, yelling doesn't bother me, profanity doesn't bother me, so I kept munching the potato chips and sour cream with cheese dip.

The hostess was practically in tears, she was so ill at ease, though.

"Maybe we could talk about something else?" I suggested.

"No, I love this, I get them going," said Eric.

"I think you're making Ellen uncomfortable," I said. I intuited this after Ellen had said, "This is making me so uncomfortable," about three times.

"This reminds me of that time at Home Depot," she said quietly to her husband.

"She tends to go off and look at things in stores and I like to just get what I came for and then leave," he said, starting to defend himself. It sounded like the usual definitions of masculinity and femininity to me so far.

"I was wearing overalls and he grabbed the tab on the side— the loop that would hold a hammer—and physically held me back from walking down one of the aisles, so I screamed," she said. "I knew he would let me go because of what people would think."

I would think it would have been the weight of that rock on her finger keeping her from wandering too far in Home Depot, and in a way I guess it was.

We had decided to barbecue brats and onions at the condo instead of the beach, which made Eric's empty cooler look like good solid foresight. We sat on the treeless communal patio. You could smell the heat coming off the cement. Two beautifully tanned gay men sat at a table near us and ate crostini.

"So what do you do, Amy?" said the liberal. It was the first time any of the guys including Eric had addressed me all day.

"I used to be a pop-culture critic but now I'm unemployed," I said.

"Wow, that's—"

"She's got a Fender Strat," Eric cut him off.

The liberal turned to Eric. "You know, if you hope to be a major player, you have to take things up a notch. You should be at the *Seattle Times* and then *Rolling Stone*, not the podunk little paper you're at."

Upstairs, back in the air-conditioning, we started our good-byes. The guys yelled to the liberal about his bowel movements while he was having them. Thankfully the bathroom door was closed at least. "Whoowee! Turn that fan on," Eric said, waving his hand under his nose while the lawyer put yellow crime-scene tape over the door so the liberal couldn't get out of the bathroom.

"We promised ourselves we'd stop acting this way when we turned thirty."

"Let's make it thirty-five," they said, high-fiving each other.

I would have liked to offer Ellen more than just the name of a great sushi restaurant downtown. I would have liked to offer her my friendship. She would need all the women friends she could get to dilute this particular man show.

I had a feeling—call it feminine intuition—that I wouldn't be dating Eric again, so as the liberal yelled his good-byes through the bathroom door, I gave her the address of a place on First with great sashimi and left it at that.

BUNK DEBUNK

Myth: It's a man's world (and they start 'em young). (Part II)

Bunked!

When I was in fourth grade, the girls in our class put together a play we had written. When I look back on it, it was actually quite a clever premise. We each played a different character from literature, unrelated to one another, and threw them together to see how they'd interact. The end result was Snow White discussing her views on the Seven Dwarfs with Alice in Wonderland, who in turn would enlighten her on the whole rabbit-hole situation.

It was free-flowing and impromptu and at one point we danced through the aisle we had made with the classroom chairs. Our audience—the boys in class—punched and pinched us as we passed, effectively ending our performance. Later, our reviews were harsher than a bad off-Broadway play being trounced by the *New York Times*. Our teacher angrily asked us what we were thinking walking through a male audience. Did we expect to *not* be punched and pinched?

When I was twelve or thirteen, the kids in the cafeteria used to chant, "Ritchie, Ritchie, Ritchie," because it was the last name of one of the school lunch ladies. I guess we didn't like her, although I've honestly never been a big fan of ganging up on someone or name calling. I can't remember my role, but as usual I was probably some sort of clueless bystander. What I do remember is that the school sent a letter to my parents stating that two tables—one of boys, one of girls—in the cafeteria were chanting during lunch and that it was very upsetting for Mrs. Ritchie. (Mrs. Ritchie.

Amazing who could get married back in the '70s, by the way. I know women who look like supermodels and own their own companies, yet can't get a date to save their lives. Apparently "the zeros" is social commentary as well as a decade marker, but I digress . . .)

My parents laughed hysterically, framed the reprimand letter, and hung it on the wall in their bedroom. I was pissed though. The letter clearly stated that there were two sexes to blame, yet the word all over the newly quiet cafeteria the next day was that only the girls' parents got the letter. I guess the school district really took the old "boys will be boys and are prone to chant stuff" saying to heart.

When I was a sophomore in high school, we all had to take a class entitled "hygiene," a surprisingly boring euphemism for "sex and drugs." Along with really dull clinical analysis of the stuff many students were ingesting at their lockers, we were informed by our gym teacher–drug counselor–sex therapist that "when things get hot in the backseat, it's the girl's responsibility to control the situation, because boys can't." (The news that sophomore girls were the ones who had to bear all burden of sexual responsibility was joyfully embraced by several members of the faculty, by the way.)

I wonder what my Web site would be if it were called Dating Andy? I'm thinking it would include a whole lotta sex and that the letters I get would start "You stud . . ." instead of "Don't you feel slutty having dinner with two different men in the same week?"

DATE 48 Harry Potter and the Fellini Extras

TRUE CONFESSION

I was starting to get annoyed with the whole arts lifestyle, maybe for the first time in my life.

Harry booked me in advance for a date at an art space he knew of in Capitol Hill. As inspired as he is about art and creativity, it's often followed by the earthy thud of his cheapness. "You can look up their Web site to find out more about the place," he said. *Considerate, if slightly unusual for someone who doesn't even own a computer,* I thought. Then predictably: "They have a password you can get for a 10 percent discount on food and drinks there." Coming from him, it wasn't something mentioned in passing, it was a request.

He had told me we could bring our own art projects to the bar to work on. He brought a lamp he was making, but since my only art is writing, I just put a pen in my purse.

"God, look at me," Harry said. "When I was in high school I used to take so much pride in my appearance, now I'm wearing overalls with paint on them and I just realized my shirt is on inside out."

As we walked the few blocks from the car to the club, we passed cars or what used to be cars—one covered in round mirrors, one covered in artificial flowers like a Buick floral explosion. Outside of the entrance a young couple was fighting—physically fighting. I thought they were kidding, but it was hard to tell.

We walked into a big, open space with tables and booths along the wall, a small stage, a bar at the far end, and lamps and art designed by previous patrons.

"I'll buy you a drink," Harry said.

At the bar a man who looked like the lead in *The Crying Game* ordered a greyhound. I told him with authority that it was invented in 1901 at the Roosevelt Hotel in L.A.

"Really?" He and Harry were impressed.

"Oh, I have no idea, I just made that up," I said.

Harry and I both ordered gin and tonics. We slid into a red vinyl booth against a wall and he worked on the lamp he was decorating to go with the rest of his Bizarre Animals of Whimsy found-objects series. I just sat and watched him work. I was starving and the gin went right to my head. I wanted something to eat, but as always with Harry I didn't feel free to order and also as always I only had a few dollars on me.

"When I was in art school I used to do smash sketches," he said. "You have a model and do a really quick drawing, tear off the sheet, do another, tear that off. I like it, it's macho."

"I should do that with my writing," I said.

Smash sketches. I didn't have the nerve to tell him I do smash dating. A quick profile and then tear it off and start another.

"I've been writing about you," I said.

"That's cool. It's weird, I've had a couple of other people write stories about me."

"It's because you're a ready-made character."

"One girl I knew wrote about me and it got published."

"That's my goal in life."

He didn't know about the Web site, although I told men I

wasn't nearly as close to. It's always easier to reveal yourself to people when there's nothing at stake.

I turned my attention to the room. "Hey posse!" someone from the booth next to us yelled to a pair of blonde girls with black glasses. The two guys sitting there had multiplied since I last looked and now there were sixteen people. They were passing around a brown grocery bag of pears that someone had brought from their garden.

The DJ played the theme to *The Exorcist*. A wiry man swiveled a red Hula Hoop in the middle of the room while a girl in a pirate hat and a man in a kilt roller-skated around him. A female acrobat did a handstand on another's shoulders. The only traditional thing I noticed about the crowd was that the women were very young and the men were middle-aged.

I was getting a headache from the gin and some guy who sat down with us was telling an involved story about how his bicycle had been stolen. He finally left to go have a cigarette outside. The bar allows Fellini's *Satyricon*, but it doesn't allow smoking, apparently.

I couldn't take the hunger any longer and Harry was ready to go, so we decided to walk to a pizza place.

"One of my friends is really into that whole scene. Part of the time, anyway," Harry said. "He's a thirty-five-year-old software designer with an SUV and a 401k, but he does the hippie-art thing on the weekends."

"Don't you think that's a little pathetic, though?" I said, punching the walk signal on the traffic light. "Presenting himself as a free-spirited artist trapped in the lifestyle of having a house on the water and too much Microsoft stock when really he's just a horny middle-aged man who wants to ogle strung-out underage girls running around in nothing but body paint?"

Harry shrugged. "He finds it relaxing."

Typical. I call it the Opportunistic Hippie Syndrome. Some men I used to hang out with were afflicted with it too. We would be at a party and they would suggest that everyone get out of their clothes and into the hot tub, arguing that it was in the spirit of friendship and no judgment, "you know, like in the sixties."

The conversation Monday morning would be as follows:

Guy 1: I feel like I miss out because I can't wear my glasses into the hot tub.

Guy 2: You didn't miss anything, the really good-looking girls all kept their clothes on again.

In that moment, waiting for the walk sign with Harry Potter, I realized: I'm too old for this. My whole adult life I've wanted to be a working artist and I've wanted to be with a guy who was an artist but also financially stable and it didn't seem like both those qualities often peacefully coexist in the same guy. For the first time the trade-off didn't seem worth it.

We got to the pizza place just after 11:00 p.m. and they wouldn't serve us.

"That's so inconsiderate," Harry said.

"Well, they're closing," I said.

"They could still make us a salad or something," he said.

Quite a sense of entitlement for someone who claims to champion the working class. I guessed he had never worked as a waiter.

We ended up at a saloon that looked like a brothel. We headed for the bar with its stained-glass windows and smoke that was settled in like permanent fog. The place was absolutely packed and it was only a Monday night.

While I looked at the late-night happy hour menu, Harry went back to describe his car to the hostess so it wouldn't be towed from the tiny parking lot, which was for customers only.

"I drew her a picture of my car instead of describing it," he said. "She should be able to tell which one it is, though. It doesn't have a bumper."

I decided on the only thing that I felt Harry could comfortably afford: a small Caesar salad with chicken and a glass of water. It totaled $3. He had a burger and fries and a beer.

The jukebox flipped from "Like a Virgin" to "Video Killed the Radio Star."

When the check came, he told me I could just leave the tip. It equaled the cost of my meal.

DATE 49 Harry Potter and the Last Supper

TRUE CONFESSION

As it turns out, I'm really not cut out for this dating-more-than-one-man thing after all.

He was forty-five minutes late.

"You're forty-five minutes late."

"Listen to you, 'You're forty-five minutes late.'" He laughed, mimicking me. "What does time matter?"

Harry Potter was having dinner at my house. The night before he had mentioned that he and his landlord had ripped out his kitchen to expand his apartment, so I of course invited him over for a home-cooked meal. He brought a fairly expensive bottle of red wine, a nice merlot. He sat at the Cheetos-yellow kitchen table at which I write but don't use for meals unless I'm eating at my laptop, which is usually, now that I think of it.

I doused some chicken breasts with soy sauce, garlic, and ginger and threw them under the broiler. I cracked open a container of hummus and put it out with a bag of baby carrots as an hors d'oeuvre (Harry told me he once ate so many of these that he was convinced his skin was turning orange) and tossed some red bell pepper and sweet red onions in olive oil and put them under the broiler too.

He picked up the brochure I had brought home from the van Gogh to Mondrian exhibit I had seen with Eric Van Halen. "I went to this, too," he said. I was surprised he would spend the money for even the greats since he is so poor. "My friend and his girlfriend took me so I could narrate, use my degree in art history and all. I didn't like it."

"Didn't like van Gogh?"

"Didn't like going out with them, they're into PDA and I'm not, even for myself. I dunno."

"Plus it was a Saturday night," I said.

"What does that matter? The art was great, though. They like taking me because I say things that you can't get on the headsets. Like . . . I like seeing what the artist must have been like in his studio, the anthropology of his daily life. I noticed on one painting van Gogh had used thick slabs of paint, but they were flattened. That's because he was working so fast that he did another painting and stacked it on top of it before it was dry. I love that kind of thing."

"I can see your anthropology here," he said, running his hand over a spot on one of the table's legs where the bright orange yellow had worn through to its original white.

"Yeah, I guess I rub my foot against it as I'm writing," I said.

"If this table were in a museum, people who are born two hundred years from now could be trying to figure you out."

We ate at the coffee table in my living room, sitting on the hardwood floor with our backs against the couch. The chicken was juicy and good.

We climbed off the floor onto the couch and had bowls of vanilla ice cream with chunks of ginger in it. The chicken had ginger in it too. "It's too much fresh ginger for one meal," I said.

"No, I love it," said Harry.

After more wine . . .

"That's the dumbest thing I've ever heard."

"Why else would young girls be fixated on horses? It's because they make them feel good."

"You and Todd think that teenage girls like horses because riding them is like sex."

"Yeah, that's why we call each other Nibbles and Applemunch."

Harry leaned back on my couch, apparently resting his case, and took a drink of the red wine.

"You call each other made-up horse names so that underage girls will want to ride you? I had a pony when I was growing up. Her name was Cocoa and our relationship wasn't at all sexual, at least not for me."

"These are the kinds of things Todd and I talk about when we meet for coffee every morning."

"Sounds like you've got a real Algonquin Roundtable going on there. Hey, did you ever finish doing the interior of his house?"

"Yeah, I'm painting some place in Bellevue now. I smoke a pipe while I work just for the effect. I'm charging them so much I should at least *look* like a craftsman."

"Your apartment is free, your paintings sell for seven hundred dollars, your clients are rich . . . how come you never have money?"

"I have lots of money. I could afford a Mercedes if I wanted. I just don't like to spend anything."

The ducking into the bathroom to avoid paying for coffee, the hanging back at the Japanese gardens so I would buy the tickets, asking me to throw in $4 for a salad at a bar during happy hour. It's one thing to be a starving artist; it's wholly another to pretend to be one. He didn't have a bathroom in his apartment, for God's sake, he shared one down the hall.

"So you could totally be the guy in the nice house who picks up the check."

"I could, but that's not me. That's not who I am."

He chose that moment to kiss me for the first time.

Maybe I shouldn't have been so hasty and rigid about things with Teflon. Did he owe me a commitment so soon? It bothered me, though. It was weird to not have him be crazy about me. It's always that way, though. When I'm interested in a guy, time slows to a crawl when I'm not hearing from him. I notice every little thing he does or doesn't do. I'm insane. When I'm not into someone, I don't even notice which nights I'm seeing him. I'm the coolest, most patient, unruffled girlfriend ever, only because I'm not seeing myself as his girlfriend. It's sick really. By definition I never really get what I want because the guy I'm the most crazy about will likely be driven away. I can have the undying affection of the one I don't care for though.

My own personal theory is that the more desirable men know they're more sought after and are therefore more difficult to pin down. Of course guys who aren't good looking or well-employed or charming are available. Where are they going to go? A sought-after man has so many options.

I realized that for the first time in my life I definitely wasn't dating for fun anymore. I was really looking at what a man had to offer long term and it wasn't pretty. Harry Potter was funny and one of the most interesting men I knew, I felt comfortable with him, but there was the poverty thing which had horrifyingly morphed into the new fake-poverty thing. Oh, plus Nibbles and Applemunch.

Teflon had a lot to offer long term. Certainly materially he had a great lifestyle. His kisses were perfect. He was fun to do nothing with. He was the first person in my life I had ever had sexual chemistry with who was actually appropriate for me. He wasn't crazy enough about me, though. There was the e-mail-only communication, his Spock-like quality; he actually told me once while we were in the throes of passion that he didn't "parse that information" when I was talking dirty.

Harry interrupted my thoughts.

"The first time I kiss someone I think 'I have successfully kissed this person.' So what did you think?" he said.

"I had fun," I said.

"Is that all you're going to give me?"

"Yes."

I shut the door behind him and took a deep breath. There was a knock and Harry poked his head back in.

"I have successfully kissed this person," he said, and left again.

BUNK DEBUNK

Myth: Men don't change.

Bunked!

Otherwise known as the "doing the same person and expecting different results is the definition of insanity" theory. It's not just men, though. I think most people don't veer much from their core personality, at least not permanently. Women would save themselves a lot of grief by accepting this.

It's a little-known bit of *Star Wars* trivia that in the original version of *The Empire Strikes Back*, Yoda advises Luke Skywalker to "do or do not . . . and while you're at it, could you try to change these things about yourself, since it looks like we're going to be spending a lot of time together" and hands him a list of Luke's character flaws and annoying habits. Luke then weakly answers, "I'll try," as his eyes scan a full page of eight-point font.

Sadly, that scene was scrapped for the pithier "Do or do not. There is no try," which not only shaved almost three seconds off the film's running time, but was also more realistic, as both characters are male.

You see, men tend to either shrug and accept or just stop calling, but there isn't a biological drive to fix people—and by that I mean their women—based on perceived potential, what their friends' girlfriends are like, or which phase the moon is in. That is the realm of women.

I consider myself a masculine thinker. I love hanging out with guys. I've been in bands; I've been the only woman on editorial staffs. I see right through men . . . and I date like they do. The Web site is testimony to that. Not for me instant adoration and forsaking all others after a great first date—I'm busy getting ready for dinner with the next guy.

Yet I horrify myself when I like a man who doesn't fit me quite right and think, *Fixer-upper! I will explain to him exactly what he's doing wrong and then he can change.*

I actually start to justify it by thinking that I would be doing him a service. That if he could be a better listener, he wouldn't repeat past relationship mistakes; if he could be less sarcastic, his love life would be smoother. I mentally tell myself that I'm no different from a Jedi master—a Jedi dating master! Men can learn from my great wisdom. Then I conjure an even bigger lie: that I want to make him better for the women in his future.

I mean really, unless they're going to give me a room over the garage after they're married, what do I care?

TRUE CONFESSION

After twenty-seven dinners, seven lunches, three brunches, two coffees, four appetizers, four horror movies, one lust-inducing cornfield, and many bottles of wine, I finally found the person I was looking for.

The book Teflon had lent me on our first date, *Running with Scissors*, was still sitting on my nightstand. I had e-mailed the agent for the book. He had been very enthusiastic about my writing. I e-mailed the news to Teflon, who got back to me by his usual method of correspondence: e-mail (which I find cold) and after two days (which I also find cold). It was disheartening, since my news is never going to get much bigger than having a big New York agent interested in me. I was never going to get what I wanted from him. When I told Harry Potter about it he was thrilled—immediately and by phone. The agent then completely disappeared. How like a man. I couldn't bring myself to finish the book. Every time I walked into my bedroom it was a reminder of the two biggest failures I currently had going: my heart-wrenching relationship with Teflon and my stalled writing career. I had put off the last date for as long as I could. It was time to end it.

I invited Teflon over for dinner to say good-bye and give him back his book. He was late because a woman had backed into a man at a stop sign on my corner. That had happened to a friend of mine once and I had told Teflon about it on our first date. He didn't remember that. Although he was the only witness to the accident, I felt he was stalling about coming upstairs to my apartment. The cop who finally showed seemed to concur and dismissed him immediately.

We hadn't seen each other for a month. He didn't look good. We had had an argument about him not asking me out on Saturday nights and then I had changed my glowing date report about our dinner at his house, which offended him.

I had offered to change it back. When I was a music critic in L.A., the guys I worked with used to give good reviews based on which backup singers slept with them, but it was the first time I had ever offered to change a review for someone.

"If that's really the way you perceived that night, then don't change it on my account. I just thought it was a nicer evening than the way you depicted it," he said. "I guess I don't fully understand what you're trying to do when you write about a date. I know you want to emphasize some things for effect, since that's part of your style. I guess I'm just surprised about what things you chose to emphasize. Maybe I'm just too close to that particular date to be objective—I felt like I came off as a cheap, anal geek with bad taste in furniture and some skills at making garlic mashed potatoes. Parts of it were definitely wry and funny, but I walked away from it thinking 'Wow, that guy is a loser.'"

I was crushed. I thought he was amazing. I was so attracted to him and this was how I had handled it.

He listened to me bitch about my writing career. How it must be nice for everyone but me to seamlessly go from getting a degree to a great job, how even the dumbest receptionist is more acknowledged for her craft than I am, how I envy soulless nonartists and their nine-to-five existence and their direct deposits. How I've hit rock bottom and I'm thinking of taking a technical writing job at an insurance company.

"I know of a great Web site called Things My Girlfriend and I Have Argued About," I said. "It's basically a list of things this British writer fights with his girlfriend about. It took him seven years to get a book deal based on it, so the worst-case scenario is that I have to wait five more years."

"No, the worst-case scenario is that you never get published at all." He was right, but ouch.

"Are you done with your fifty dates?"

"I'm trying to decide how to end it. I want it to have two endings like *The French Lieutenant's Woman*."

"I haven't read it."

"I meant the movie. Half of it is in the modern day and half is a Gothic romance."

"But horror's your genre."

"I can't handle horror anymore, it's too disturbing. I've been having nightmares. Lately all I can take are romantic comedies."

I was cooking dinner for him. Chicken breasts with garlic and ginger, salad with red onions and a vinaigrette, broiled asparagus, and buttermilk chocolate cake for dessert. I was having him make the garlic mashed potatoes since we'd have to throw them away if I tried. I can whip out this meal perfectly since I make it so often, but tonight I was nervous and my game was off.

I was re-creating things from the Harry Potter dinner of a few nights before. It was relationship comparison shopping and I couldn't stop even though I saw how hollow and ridiculous I was being. I dragged out a framed picture of a Thai girl sitting in a boat that my late father painted. I keep it in a closet, not because I don't like it but because it's too dark and I think it's bad luck to have a picture of an obviously poor, obviously single woman displayed. Teflon dismissed the picture. He also dismissed the fact that I qualified for Mensa and was a dancer for fifteen years. ("Professionally?" "No, but I took lessons after school three times a week." "Oh well then . . .")

I told him about my childhood pony, Cocoa, and he only said, "You had a pony? How clichéd of you."

After he had decreed his only contribution, the garlic mashed potatoes, "the highlight of the meal," he put our dishes in the sink.

He came back and sat next to me on the couch and tugged on the hammer loop of my overalls. I was wearing them undone with a little T-shirt. They are a size too big, they rode low on my hips.

"Do you think we would have been friends if we hadn't dated?"

"I can't think of where we would have even met," he said, avoiding the question.

"A dot-com. You'd be on the technical side, I'd be on the creative."

"Is this over?" he said. He didn't look at me.

"It must be hard to be a guy," I said, avoiding the question.

"It is," he said.

"It's not over," I said, and kissed him.

We had sex, but it wasn't the same. I didn't come and he didn't care.

"So you want me to bring your cake in?" I asked as I dressed. He looked like he was thinking hard.

"No, I don't want to get chocolate crumbs in your bed."

"This cake tastes like cocoa, not chocolate," he said. I had baked the southern buttermilk cake from scratch—yes, with cocoa—and he was bitching about it. Postcoitally, I might add. It was his second cocoa diss of the evening.

"I should get going. The last bus will be leaving soon."

"You're not staying over?" I was incredulous.

"Normally I would love to, but I have to bring my car into the mechanic first thing." He was using the voice he uses when panhandlers tell him a story and he plays along with their homeless fiction: "That's great that you're starting a new job tomorrow and just need some cash for Dial soap rather than a bottle of booze. Congratulations!"

There are pivotal moments in every relationship. That point where you make a decision that can be the difference between a final good-bye and a first mortgage payment. I always go in for a hug and Teflon always goes in for a kiss. In that pivotal moment I caught his shirt with my fingers and him with a "hey" and got both, and the mechanic ended up waiting for an 8:00 a.m. client who never showed.

But that didn't happen.

What happened was that I thought about asking him if he could call instead of e-mailing and if he could be more emotional about me and if he could somehow see himself getting more serious about us, but I knew that wasn't who he was, so I didn't say anything.

He kissed me good-bye and after he shut the door I realized I had lied when I said it wasn't over. He didn't stay that night or any other night. I felt like I had the stomach flu for three days and I kept tearing up.

A few days later I got the call I had been dreaming of. The conversation that would begin the relationship I had wanted since I started the site. It was the literary agent from New York. I told myself it was all I ever wanted.

I was so sad, though. You know at fairs where a strong man takes a sledgehammer and hits the pallet so hard that it rings a bell and then he wins a prize? I had that happen with my heart, but instead of ringing, it cracked in two and then one side of it fell off and the other just sort of hung there by a wire and there was no prize. I don't know how I got so attached to someone who didn't care about me.

Harry kept calling but I just couldn't pick up. "I'm stopping by to see if you're okay," his last message finally said.

I ran down the stairs when he buzzed me. We sat on my front

steps. "I brought you something," he said, handing me a naked Barbie doll. "I went back and bought her for you that day we went to see the cherry trees. I bought myself a Ken. I'm making a lamp out of him. Look, her dates even match."

"What do you mean?"

"She's not a Frankenbarbie," he said.

Oh, no.

"I read through your site."

"But you don't even have a computer."

"Well, no, but I have a TV. You've been on the news."

"God, I'm so sorry. It was just hard to tell you especially."

"It's no big deal. I figure it's your art. First Amendment and all."

"You can force different elements with a Barbie, Amy, and even then she'll still be tall and blonde," he said. "With people there's always a trade-off."

"Yeah, I'm realizing that," I said.

We laughed.

BUNK DEBUNK

Myth: There's one perfect soul mate out there for each of us.

Debunked!

I think everyone has tons of people they'd be compatible with, so why limit yourself? You have hundreds of "soul mates."

If you don't get out there, you may only meet a few of them, though.

About the Author

A while ago a guy asked me what makes my dates so special. I was put off by this for several reasons: a) I didn't know him, b) I was on a live television talk show at the time, and c) I didn't care for his tone.

It's a good question, though. One I've thought about a lot since my love life has received so much attention from the media, people bored at work surfing the Internet, and, eventually, the New York publishing community.

Why is it more interesting when *I* go on fifty dates than when other writers go on one hundred or one thousand? Mine weren't even with all different guys, yet I think that may be the answer.

I wrote a genuine exploration of what it's like for an average person to date, not what an average writer will do to get a book deal (anything, apparently) or what an average bimbo will do to drive up traffic on a Web site (anything pornographic, apparently).

This book is not a catalog of terrible first dates designed so that hilarity ensues, although that does happen at first. It is, rather, a sincere testimony to my earnestness—and, yes, utter cluelessness—about men and relationships. You've seen me hone my skills at meeting men so that my methods go from awkward and online to effortless. You've seen me go from dating party-anecdotes to developing real relationships.

As a writer I have reviewed many other things apart from men, including pho restaurants and pop bands. Before that my jobs included professional Christmas caroling and delivering messages to the locker room of a National League Football team.

I once met Timothy Leary. We were both drinking chardonnay. He was very polite.

Amy

FIVE REASONS WHY IT'S A BAD IDEA TO WRITE ABOUT YOUR LOVE LIFE IN PUBLIC
(Narrowed Down from Ninety)

1. **Your privacy is slightly diminished.**
   You will have conversations like: "Wow, that must have been so humiliating when that guy dumped you. You really liked him. So who are you sleeping with now? My name's Peter, by the way."

2. **You'll frighten away the kind of men who don't want to date a woman who writes about her love life in public.**
   These include professional men, homeowners, men with no prison record, and men who are normal.

3. **You'll attract the kind of men who want to date a woman who writes about her love life in public.**
   Self-explanatory.

4. **You can forget about being a coy, Mata Hari–type woman of intrigue.**
   You will have conversations like:
   You: "Well, I wasn't *that* into you when we were dating."
   Him: "Obviously you were."
   You: "I don't know how you could possibly know that."
   Him: "You said it. On the Internet. You're not exactly mysterious. You should at least *play* hard to get. I mean, do you know anything at all about men?" etc.

5. **You can forget about being a modest, Jane Austen–type woman of propriety.**
   Once you've used the words "girth" and "clerk at Blockbuster Video" in the same sentence, any chance of having your blush being compared to the virginal pink of a tea rose is pretty much shot.